READINGS
in the
BOOKS
of the
APOCRYPHA

WILBERT M. VAN DYK

WESTBOW
PRESS
A DIVISION OF THOMAS NELSON
& ZONDERVAN

Copyright © 2014 Wilbert Van Dyk.

All rights reserved. No part of this book may be used or reproduced by any means, graphic, electronic, or mechanical, including photocopying, recording, taping or by any information storage retrieval system without the written permission of the publisher except in the case of brief quotations embodied in critical articles and reviews.

Except where noted all quotations are from the Kindle edition (Harper Collins, 2006) of the New Revised Standard Version Bible (NRSV), copyright 1989 the Division of Christian Education of the National Council of the Churches of Christ in the United States of America. Used by permission. All rights reserved. References marked NIV are from the NIV Study Bible, Zondervan, 1985.

WestBow Press books may be ordered through booksellers or by contacting:

WestBow Press
A Division of Thomas Nelson & Zondervan
1663 Liberty Drive
Bloomington, IN 47403
www.westbowpress.com
1 (866) 928-1240

Because of the dynamic nature of the Internet, any web addresses or links contained in this book may have changed since publication and may no longer be valid. The views expressed in this work are solely those of the author and do not necessarily reflect the views of the publisher, and the publisher hereby disclaims any responsibility for them.

Any people depicted in stock imagery provided by Thinkstock are models, and such images are being used for illustrative purposes only. Certain stock imagery © Thinkstock.

ISBN: 978-1-4908-5863-0 (sc)

Library of Congress Control Number: 2014919564

Printed in the United States of America.

WestBow Press rev. date: 11/21/2014

*Dedicated to my
children and grandchildren
who
encouraged me to put this material into writing*

Contents

The Belggic Confession ix
Preface xi
The Apocryphal Books of the Old Testament xiii
Development of the Old Testament Canon xv

The Apocalyptic Book of the Apocrypha, Part One 1
The Apocalyptic Book of the Apocrypha, Part Two 13
The Apocryphal Books of History, Part One 23
The Apocryphal Books of History, Part Two 37
The Apocryphal Books of Wisdom, Part One 49
The Apocryphal Books of Wisdom, Part Two 59
The Apocryphal Legends, Part One 69
The Apocryphal Legends, Part Two 81

The Belggic Confession[*]

Article 6. *The Difference Between Canonical and Apocryphal Books*

We distinguish between these holy books (sixty-six books are named) and the apocryphal ones, which are the third and fourth books of Esdras; the books of Judith, Tobit, Wisdom, Jesus Sirach, Baruch; what was added to the story of Esther; the Song of the Three Children in the Furnace; the story of Susanna; the story of Bel and the Dragon; the Prayer of Manasseh; and the two books of Maccabees.

The church may certainly read these books and learn from them as far as they agree with the canonical books. But they do not have such power and virtue that one could confirm from their testimony any point of faith of the Christian religion. Much less can they detract from the authority of the other holy books.

---

[*] The Belgic Confession. also known as The Confession of Faith, was written in the context of the sixteenth century Protestant Reformation. It was drafted by the Belgian pastor, Guido de Bres in 1563. It is significant because, although it does not recognize the apocryphal books as authoritative for faith and life, it does encourage believers to read these books and learn from them. Still today The Belgic Confession remains one of the confessional standards of churches in the Reformed tradition.

Preface

The fourteen books named as apocryphal in the sixteenth century Belgic Confession are traditionally understood as the Old Testament Apocrypha. The actual number in any given collection of these books may range from nine to sixteen. The number is higher when for example, the *Letter of Jeremiah* is excerpted from *Baruch*, and the *Prayer of Azariah* is excerpted from *The Song of the Three Children*. The books number less than fourteen when the *Additions to the Book of Esther* are incorporated into canonical *Esther* and the books of *The Song of the Three Children, Susanna*, and *Bel and the Dragon* are added to canonical *Daniel*. This study will name the books as they are identified in the Belgic Confession.

Full translations of the apocryphal books are widely available. After sketching the history of The Apocrypha, this study stitches together selected readings from each of the books. The result is a coherent sampling of the content and style of each book. The material that follows may be both an appetizer and a meal. As an appetizer it may whet the appetite for further reading in apocryphal literature. As a meal it may serve as a satisfying introduction to these ancient books.

The readings from The Apocrypha are in indented blocks of print.

Wilbert M. Van Dyk
Grand Rapids, Michigan 2014

The Apocryphal Books of the Old Testament

Apocryphal Books as listed in the Belgic Confession, Article 6	Books included in a Roman Catholic printing of the Bible (Douay Version, 1953)	Books as identified in the New Revised Standard Version Kindle – 2006
Third Esdras	Not included	First Esdras
Fourth Esdras	Not included	Second Esdras
Tobit	Tobias	Tobit
Judith	Judith	Judith
Wisdom	Wisdom	The Wisdom of Solomon
Jesus Sirach	Ecclesiasticus	Ecclesiasticus
Baruch	Baruch	Baruch
		Letter of Jeremiah (Baruch 6)
Addendum to Esther	Included in Esther	Additions to the Book of Esther
Song of the Three Children	Included in Daniel	Prayer of Azariah (1st part of book) The Song of the Three Jews
Story of Susanna	Included in Daniel	Susanna

Story of Bel and the Dragon	Included in Daniel	Bel and the Dragon
Prayer of Manasseh	Nor included	The Prayer of Manasseh
First Maccabees	I Maccabees	First Maccabees
Second Maccabees	2 Maccabees	Second Maccabees

Note 1: The first Douay version appeared in 1609-1610 as an English translation of the *Latin Vulgate*.

Note 2: Some NRSV's include the Apocrypha, either as a unit between the Testaments or in their Old Testament sequence.

Development of the Old Testament Canon

In the beginning there were no books. Among the ancestors of the people who would live in the land of Canaan the great stories of creation, Noah, and Abraham were told by parents to their children. Early in human history people found a way to put the sounds that they heard into symbols that they could see. On clay tablets. On papyrus scrolls. And books were born: books of law by Moses, books of history by Ezra, Psalms by David, prophecy by Jeremiah.

Eventually, by our count, there were 39 of them, mostly in the Hebrew language, written by and for the Hebrew people who believed that these books were a record of God at work among them. In these books God was speaking, God was directing, God was promising. There was no question. These books were God's word. They were the sacred Scriptures of the Jews.

But were they the only Scriptures? Did God reveal himself to his people only in these Hebrew books from Genesis to Malachi? The question became important about a hundred years after the time of Malachi when some Greek books began to surface. That happened shortly before 300 B.C. when Alexander the Great conquered Palestine and its neighbors and introduced Greek language and Greek culture. Some of these new books that were written in Greek elaborated on familiar stories already told in the Hebrew books. Some of them put words into the mouths of the heroes of faith. Still others recorded important historical events. But were they also to be received as God's word? The people knew that God spoke Hebrew. But did he also speak in Greek?

The question was troubling because in these Greek books God was not always presented as the primary character. The people knew that God was always at work in his world, but in these newer books recognition of him was muted. The people missed the "this is what the Lord says" of the law and the prophets.

The Council of Jamnia

That uncertainty over which books were God's authoritative word for Israel continued until 90 A.D. when a Council of Jewish scholars was convened at the rabbinical school in the city of Jamnia, near the site of today's Tel Aviv. The scholars did not focus on rejecting certain books. The focus of Jamnia was rather on identifying those books that bore the stamp of divine revelation.

The Council began with the first five books of the Bible, the books of law. Clearly, those books were God's word. Equally obvious were the prophets who spoke God's word to the people. The history books told of God building his kingdom in Israel with the continuing interplay between the kings and the prophets. The writings, like the Psalms, were expressions of covenant people living in communion with their covenant God. The rabbis struggled with some of the books, like Ecclesiastes, the Song of Solomon, and Job. But one by one the books of the Hebrew Scripture were recognized as God revealing himself and his will for his people. One by one what we know as the thirty-nine books of the Old Testament were accepted as divine authority for faith and life. From Genesis to Malachi God was making himself known.

So the Old Testament canon was established. What the Council of Jamnia concluded was no surprise to the faithful Jews. Jamnia simply confirmed what they always knew: the Hebrew Scripture and only that Scripture was God's word. Still today both the Jewish synagogue and the Christian church live with the decision of Jamnia. The thirty-nine books from Genesis to Malachi: this is God's word.

The Apocrypha

What about those other books that told stories about biblical people and events? The Council of Jamnia did not put those Greek books into a separate category and decide to reject them. Jamnia simply found that in those books God was not revealing himself, at least not as clearly as he did in the Hebrew Scriptures.

Those Greek apocryphal books continued to be good reading. Some of them showed genuine Jewish piety. Others glorified some of the heroes of faith, or reflected on familiar Old Testament teachings. Still others filled in good information about the history of life in Palestine during the inter-testamental period.

Eventually these books became known as "apocryphal" from a Greek word technically meaning "hidden." They were known as apocryphal because the quality of divine revelation was not clear in these books. More recently the word "apocryphal" has been nuanced to mean "of uncertain origin or authority."

The phrase "The Books of the Apocrypha" identifies a collection of fourteen books that relate to ideas, people, or events that are recorded in the Old Testament. These fourteen books are not the only apocryphal works. In all, late Judaism and early Christianity dealt with more than seventy books that fit this category, including the "Book of Enoch" that Jude referenced in his letter, verses 14-15. But historically the fourteen emerged as The Books of The Apocrypha. Sometimes the fourteen are combined into as few as nine books, other times they are divided into as many as sixteen books.

All of the Books of the Apocrypha were written between 300 B.C. and late in the first century A.D. Most of them were written by anonymous authors who wrote in the Greek language. Most of these books are imaginary accounts of what the author thought might have happened several centuries earlier. Eventually most of them were adopted as authoritative by the Roman Catholic Church. None of them were approved as authoritative for faith and life by the churches of the Protestant Reformation. All of these books provide helpful insights into Jewish religious practices, personal piety, culture, and history during the inter-testamental period, the four hundred years between the prophet Malachi and the beginning of the New Testament.

About a hundred years after Alexander the Great had introduced the Greek language into the area a group of Jewish scholars in northern Egypt began the process of translating the Hebrew Scriptures into the Greek language. By that time several books that related to Old Testament history were already available in Greek. It was not surprising therefore that those newer books found a home in this Greek translation, known at the *Septuagint*.

By the time of Christ, Rome had become the major world power and the Latin language soon replaced the Greek language as the language of the church. Around 400 A.D. Saint Jerome took on the enormous task of translating the Hebrew Old Testament and the Greek New Testament into the Latin language. This translation was known as *The Latin Vulgate*. In this translation Jerome included several of the Greek books, but marked that material as "apocryphal" to distinguish it from the "canonical" books.

For about 1200 years Jerome's *Latin Vulgate* was unofficially accepted as the Bible of the church. Gradually the Vulgate's distinction between "apocryphal" and "canonical" faded until all of Jerome's Vulgate was widely accepted as the divinely inspired and authoritative word of God. During these centuries the church developed certain religious practices such as the giving of alms and other good works as necessary for salvation as well as prayers for the dead to hasten them through their time of purging. The church found "biblical" justification for some of these practices in the apocryphal material that had been incorporated into the flow of the Old Testament.

The Protestant Reformation

The sixteenth century saw the birth of the Protestant Reformation. Central to the conviction of the Reformers was the slogan "sola scriptura." Only Scripture. By "scripture" the Reformers meant the twenty-seven books of the New Testament, and the thirty-nine books of the Hebrew Old Testament that had been identified centuries before at the Council of Jamnia. These books were the Word of God, the Bible, the only authority for faith and life. The apocryphal additions were collected into a separate category in order to return the scriptures to their original canon.

In its response to the Protestant Reformation, the Roman Catholic Church met at the Council of Trent in 1546. One of the decisions made at that Council was to adopt the *Latin Vulgate* as the official Bible of Roman Catholicism, thereby declaring that what had been considered as apocryphal was now to be considered as authoritative as any of the other books of the Bible

In 2014 a Protestant website (gotquesstions.org) stated that the Church of Rome added books to the original scriptures. A Roman Catholic website (grottopress.org) stated that the Protestant Reformers took some books out of the Bible. There is a sense, of course, in which both are true. The Protestant Reformers took out of the *Latin Vulgate* material that Jerome had acknowledged as apocryphal. Roman Catholicism added books to the original canon when it adopted the *Latin Vulgate* as its official version of Scripture, thus making what had been considered apocryphal now to be a part of the biblical canon.

In 1609-1610 scholars in England and France translated the *Latin Vulgate* into English. This is known as the Douay-Rheims version of Scripture. It became as closely identified with Roman Catholicism as the King James Version was with Protestantism. Today a typical Protestant printing of the Bible will consist of the thirty-nine books of the Old Testament and the twenty-seven books of the New Testament. The Apocrypha, if it appears at all, will likely be located between the two testaments and clearly marked as apocryphal. A typical Roman Catholic printing of the Bible will consist of the twenty-seven books of the New Testament. The Old Testament, however, will be longer. The Douay Old Testament, for example, consists of multi-chapter additions to the books of Esther and Daniel, and several individually named books for a total of forty-six books.

The historically recognized fourteen books of the Apocrypha can be divided into four kinds of literature. One of the books is apocalyptic in nature, consisting of visions and symbols that relate to God's judgment. There are six apocryphal books of history. They will be followed by the two books of wisdom. The final category consists of the five apocryphal legends.

Things to Think About

When the Council of Jamnia (90 A.D) met the determining question was "has God revealed himself in these books?" Only a "yes" answer to that question qualified the book to be named as the authoritative word of God. In which book or books of the Bible do you think God reveals himself most clearly? What does God tell you about himself in that book, or those books?

In some books of the Bible God's self-revelation seems rather obscure. Think of books like Esther, The Song of Solomon, Ecclesiastes, and even the Letter of James. Is God revealing himself in these books? If not, do you have any idea why the church has included them? And if God does reveal himself in these books, how does he do so?

How does God make himself known to us today? Think of his revelation in Jesus Christ, in the Bible, in the work of the Holy Spirit, in creation, in his unfolding plan in your life. Where do you find the most helpful information about who God is and what he wants for you?

Have you ever heard God speak directly to you? If so, and if someone else also claimed to have heard the voice of God, but speaking a different message, how would you resolve that difference?

THE APOCALYPTIC BOOK OF THE APOCRYPHA, PART ONE

Fourth Esdras

The name "Esdras" is the Greek way of saying the Hebrew "Ezra." In its listing of the apocryphal books the *Belgic Confession* names Third and Fourth Esdras. The *New Revised Standard Version* of the Bible names those same two books First and Second Esdras.

The difference lies in how the biblical books are named. Since Ezra wrote both Ezra and Nehemiah, these two books are sometimes labeled First Ezra and Second Ezra. In that case when two apocryphal authors wanted to add to the Ezra literature, their books became Third Esdras and Fourth Esdras. But if the canonical books bear the names of Ezra and Nehemiah, then the apocryphal additions become First Esdras and Second Esdras.

These two apocryphal books were written by different authors separated by more than one hundred years of history. Fourth Esdras was written towards the end of the first century A.D., around the time that the Apostle John was writing the book of Revelation. Fourth Esdras is the only book of the Apocrypha that was written after the birth of Christ. Third Esdras was written around 50 B.C.

Neither Fourth Esdras nor Third Esdras has been accepted as authoritative by the Roman Catholic Church.

Canonical Ezra was a priest. His people had been deported into Babylonian captivity. That began in 584 B.C. Almost seven hundred years later an anonymous author imagined what must have been going on in Ezra's mind during that difficult time in Israel's history. It was not hard for Fourth Esdras to imagine Ezra in the conquest by Babylon because in the year 70 A.D. the temple in Jerusalem had been destroyed by Roman conquest. As Babylon had been part of Ezra's story, so Rome was part of the story of Esdras. The troubling question was: why did a good God allow such devastation to be visited on his covenant people? The apocryphal Esdras did not write about Rome. He wrote about Babylon because he imagined that he was the canonical Ezra in his Babylonian captivity.

The canonical book of Ezra does not record his experiences in Babylon. The book rather begins with the return of some of the exiles to Jerusalem and the daunting task of restoring the temple as a place of sacrifices and festivals. Apocryphal Esdras begins by rehearsing God's care for Israel, their disobedience, and God's judgment on them that brought them into their Babylonian captivity.

The Visions

After the first two chapters of historical reflection on God's mercy and Israel's sin, the next fourteen chapters become apocalyptic. The material consists of visions, symbols, descriptions of the final judgment and what will happen on earth before that great final day of history.

Esdras had seven visions. The first three are prayers in which Esdras talks with the angel Uriel about the apparent injustice of

Israel's Babylonian captivity and the mystery of God's final judgment at the end of time. Visions four, five, and six are a bit like the second half of the book of Daniel and some of the material in the book of Revelation. The visions feature dramatic symbolism that moves Esdras to ask Uriel for interpretation. In the final vision God gives Esdras permission to write the things that he has seen and heard.

Vision One

In his first vision Esdras was troubled by the apparent injustice in which God used the wicked Babylonians to take captive the covenant people of Israel. Esdras stated his problem.

> Then I said in my heart, Are the deeds of those who inhabit Babylon any better? Is that why it has gained dominion over Zion? For when I came here [to Babylon] I saw ungodly deeds without number, and my soul has seen many sinners during these thirty years. And my heart failed me, because I have seen how you [God] endure those who sin and have spared those who act wickedly, and have destroyed your people, and have protected your enemies, and have not shown to anyone how your way may be comprehended. Are the deeds of Babylon better than those of Zion? Or has another nation known you besides Israel? What tribes have so believed the covenants as those tribes of Jacob? Yet their reward has not appeared and their labor has borne no fruit. (3:28-33a)

The angel did not solve Esdras' problem, but challenged him by asking, "Do you think you can comprehend the way of the Most High?" (4:2) Esdras arrogantly responded, "Yes, I can." So the angel gave him a test to challenge Esdras' assumption that he could understand God.

> I [Esdras] said, "Speak, my Lord." And he said to me, "Go, weigh for me the weight of fire and measure for me a blast of wind, or call back for me the day that is past." I answered and said, "Who of those that have been born can do that, that you should ask me about such things?" (4:5-6)

So the angel made his point by telling Esdras a parable.

> He answered me and said, "I went into a forest of trees of the plain, and they made a plan, and they said, 'Come, let us go and make war against the sea so that it may recede before us and so that we may make for ourselves more forests.' In like manner the waves of the sea made a plan and said, 'Come, let us go up and subdue the forest of the plain so that there also we may have more territory for ourselves.' But the plan of the forest was in vain, for the fire came and consumed it; likewise also the plan of the waves of the sea was in vain, for the sand stood firm and blocked it. If now you were a judge between them, which would you undertake to justify, and which to condemn?" (4:13-18)

Esdras responded to the parable by declaring that both the sea and the forest had made a foolish plan because the forest is appointed to the land, and the sea is held back by the sand. And then the angel answered with these words:

> You have judged rightly, but why have you not judged so in your own case? For as the land has been assigned to the forest and the sea to its waves, so also those who inhabit the earth can only understand what is on the earth, and he who is above the heavens can understand what is above the height of the heavens. (4:20-21)

In the rest of this first vision Esdras acknowledged that when this sinful age ends and the new age comes, then the mystery of God's ways will be made known. Esdras wanted to know whether he would live to see that great day of final judgment. The angel responded by saying that he doesn't know either, because it has not been revealed to him.

Vision Two

Esdras' second vision wonders about God's judgment both in the present and at the end of time. The vision consists of three parts. In the first part, Esdras returned to the problem of his first vision. If God had chosen Israel to be his own covenant people, why did he send them into their Babylonian captivity?

The second part of the vision is perhaps the most fascinating. Esdras observed that God has placed all humanity under his judgment because of Adam's sin. And since, in the end, all humanity will be judged by God, then why didn't God create all of humanity at once to be judged at once, rather than spreading out his justice over centuries of time? A snippet of conversation gives us the flavor of Esdras' request.

> Then I answered and said, "Could you not have created at one time those who have been and those who are and those who will be so that you might show your judgment sooner?"
>
> He replied to me and said, "The creation cannot move faster than the Creator, nor can the world hold at one time those who have been created in it."
>
> I said, "How have you said to your servant that you will certainly give life at one time to your creation? If therefore all creatures will live at one time and the creation will sustain them, it might even now be able to support all of them present at one time."
>
> He said to me, "Ask a woman's womb, and say to it, 'If you bear ten children, why one after another? Request it therefore to produce ten at one time.'"
>
> And I said, 'Of course it cannot, but only each in its own time."
>
> He said to me, "Even so I have given the womb of the earth to those who from time to time are sown in it. For as an infant does not bring forth, and a woman who has become old does not bring forth

any longer, so I have made the same rule for the world that I created." (5:43-49)

In the third part of the vision, Esdras repeatedly asked the angel when the final judgment will come, and what will be the signs that precede the end. The angel responded in dramatic language about natural disaster, wondrous signs, and hostility among the people on earth. The vision ends with a message of hope in which the angel assumed the voice of God.

> It shall be that whoever remains after all that I have foretold to you shall be saved and shall see my salvation and the end of my world. And they shall see those who were taken up, who from their birth have not tasted death, and the heart of the earth's inhabitants shall be changed and converted to a different spirit. For evil shall be blotted out, and deceit shall be quenched; faithfulness shall flourish, and corruption shall be overcome, and the truth, which has been so long without fruit, shall be revealed. (6:25-28)

The angel's discourse about the signs of the times and the final judgment bears some resemblance to the New Testament, suggesting that this anonymous author in the late first century A.D. was familiar with the teachings of Jesus.

Vision Three

In this lengthy third vision Esdras was troubled by the fact that the vast number of Adam's descendants will not be saved and therefore will fall under God's final judgment. At one point Esdras even envied the animals because they will not be brought into judgment. The angel acknowledged that the way into the City of God is difficult, but the reward is great. In language that reflected Esdras' familiarity with the life and teachings of Jesus, the angel described the Messianic kingdom. In response to Esdras' curiosity the angel explained what happens at the time of death. The vision ends with an extensive description of "signs of the times," which is followed by Esdras' earnest prayer for the mercy of God on behalf of the ungodly. Throughout the vision, the angel spoke as if he were the voice of God.

The vision begins as Esdras remembered that although God created the world good, because of Adam's sin all people now stand under God's judgment. Esdras wondered whether anybody can be saved. In his Sermon on the Mount Jesus said, "Small is the gate and narrow the road that leads to life, and only a few find it." (Matthew 7:14 NIV) The angel Uriel described it this way.

> There is a city built and set on a plain, and it is full of good things, but the entrance to it is narrow and set in a precipitous place, so that there is fire on the right hand and deep water on the left. There is only one path lying between them, that is, between the fire and the water, so that only one person can walk on the path. If now the city is given to someone as an inheritance, how will the heir receive the

inheritance unless by passing through the appointed danger? (7:6- 9)

As Esdras thought about the difficulties of entering the city of God it dawned on him that although the righteous suffer difficulties now, they do so with the hope of eventual glory, whereas whatever difficulties the unrighteous may endure now will only be surpassed by the greater difficulties yet to come.

> Then I answered and said, "O sovereign Lord, you have ordained in your law that the righteous shall inherit these things, but that the ungodly shall perish. The righteous, therefore, can face difficult circumstances without hoping for easier ones, but those who have done wickedly have suffered the difficult circumstances and will never see the easier ones." (7:17-18)

The angel then went on to describe what is yet to come. In this part of the vision Esdras heard Uriel's description of the Messianic age. The language reflects elements of New Testament eschatology, but hardly provides a coherent picture of the Christian's hope.

> For indeed the time will come, when the signs that I have foretold to you will come to pass, that the city that now is not seen shall appear, and the land that now is hidden shall be disclosed. Everyone who has been delivered from the evils that I have foretold shall see my wonders. For my son the Messiah shall be revealed with those who are with him, and those who remain shall rejoice four hundred years. After

those years my son the Messiah shall die, and all who draw human breath. (7:26-29)

After seven days the world that is not yet awake shall be roused, and that which is corruptible shall perish. Then earth shall give up those who are asleep in it, and the dust those who rest there in silence, and the chambers shall give up those souls that have been committed to them. The Most High shall be revealed on the seat of judgment, and compassion shall pass away and patience shall be withdrawn. (7:31-33)

But before that day of final judgment comes to pass, we die. What happens to us at the moment of death? Esdras wanted to know whether "we shall be kept in rest until those times come when he [God] will renew the creation, or whether we shall be tormented at once." (7:75) Uriel responded.

When the decisive decree has gone out from the Most High that a person should die, as the spirit leaves the body to return again to him who gave it, first of all it adores the glory of the Most High. If it is one of those who have shown scorn and have not kept the way of the Most High, who have despised his law and hated those who fear God – such spirits shall not enter into habitations, but all shall immediately wander about in torments, always grieving and sad. (7:78-80)

And what about those who have "kept the ways of the Most High"?

> First of all, they shall see with great joy the glory of him who receives them, and they shall have rest. (7:91)

In his vision Esdras was deeply concerned about the state of those who have died in their sin to await the everlasting judgment of God. He wondered whether "on the day of judgment the righteous will be able to intercede for the ungodly, or to entreat the Most High for them." (7:102) Uriel responded.

> The Day of Judgment is decisive and displays to all the seal of truth. Just as now a father does not send his son, or a master his servant, or a friend his dearest friend to be ill or eat or sleep or be healed in his place, so no one shall ever pray for another on that day, neither shall anyone lay a burden on another, for then all shall bear their own righteousness or unrighteousness. (7:104b-105)

The angel thus rejected the idea that the prayers of the righteous may have merit to secure heaven for the unrighteous, and as such disqualifies Fourth Esdras as part of the canon of Roman Catholicism. It is interesting to note that II Maccabees 12:45 endorses the very concept that Fourth Esdras rejects.

Things to Think About

It was a problem for the Psalmist (73:12); it was a problem for Job (7:4-6); it was a problem for Habakkuk (1:1-4); it was the problem of the anonymous Esdras; it is the problem of many Christians today: why does an all-loving and all-powerful God allow his beloved children to suffer – especially often at the hands of the ungodly? How do you respond to that question?

The angel told apocryphal Esdras that the way into God's city is narrow and dangerous. John Bunyan's pilgrim (*Pilgrim's Progress*) faced all kinds of obstacles on his way to the heavenly city. Why is it difficult to be a faithful disciple of Christ? Do you find the road to eternal glory narrow and difficult? If so, in what way? And how do you cope with that?

The angel Uriel told Esdras that the prayers of the righteous do not earn eternal bliss for the unrighteous who have died. If your Christian loved ones have gone to be with the Lord, do you ever pray that they may be having joy in the presence of Christ? If so, why do we "pray for the dead" when we know that they are already blessed forevermore?

The Apocalyptic Book of the Apocrypha, Part Two

The character of the visions of the apocryphal Esdras changes with the fourth vision. In the first three visions Esdras was preoccupied with God's justice and his judgments on sinful humanity. In the next three visions Esdras saw symbolic creatures and events in the pattern of the canonical books of Daniel and Revelation.

Vision Four

In his fourth vision Esdras saw a woman who had been barren for thirty years. Night and day she prayed for a child. Finally, she gave birth to a son, the joy of her life. When he was old enough, the boy was married, but on the day of his marriage he died. Neighbors tried to comfort her, but she was inconsolable. In her grief she left town and went out to the fields, weeping shamelessly, determined to stay there until she died.

In words that may appear to be harsh, Esdras rebuked the woman for her grief. His point was that the woman grieved over the death of one son, but the world and the church (which he called

Zion) should grieve much more heavily over the multitudes that are on the road to everlasting death..

> You most foolish of women, do you not see our mourning, and what has happened to us? For Zion, the mother of us all is in deep grief and great distress. It is most appropriate to mourn now, because we are all mourning, and to be sorrowful, because we are all sorrowing; you are sorrowing for one son, but we, the whole world, for our mother. Now ask the earth and she will tell you it is she who ought to mourn over so many who have come into being upon her. From the beginning all have been born of her, and others will come, and, lo, almost all go to perdition, and a multitude of them will come to doom. (10:6-10)

As Esdras continued speaking with the woman about these things he suddenly saw a bright light, heard a great sound, the woman vanished and in her place Esdras saw a "city that was being built." (10:27) He asked the angel Uriel to interpret the vision for him.

> The woman whom you saw is Zion, which you now behold as a city being built. And as for her telling you that she was barren for thirty years, the reason is that there were three thousand years in the world before any offering was offered in it. And after three thousand years Solomon built the city, and offered offerings; and then it was that the barren woman bore a son. And as for her telling

> you that she brought him up with much care, that was the period of residence in Jerusalem. And as for her saying to you, "My son died as he entered his wedding chamber," and that misfortune had befallen her, that was the destruction that befell Jerusalem. (10:44-48)

The symbolism of the three thousand years and Solomon may be difficult to unravel. But the angel made clear that the vision about the weeping woman was about God's people Israel, Zion. The covenant people had abundant reason to grieve, particularly over the destruction of Jerusalem under the Babylonians in the time of the canonical Ezra, and under the Romans in the days of apocryphal Esdras.

<u>Vision Five</u>

The symbolism of the fifth vision shows us the rise and fall of great nations on earth, and the final victory of the kingdom of God. Esdras saw a vision of an eagle that was overcome by a lion.

> On the second night I had a vision: I saw rising from the sea an eagle that had twelve feathered wings and three heads. I saw it spread its wings over the whole earth, and all the winds of heaven blew upon it, and clouds were gathered around it. (11:1-2)

> Then I saw that the eagle flew with its wings, and reigned over the earth and over those who inhabit it. And I saw that all things under heaven were

subjected to it, and no one spoke against it – not a single creature that was on the earth. (11:5-6)

The wings and heads of this great eagle represented the kingdoms of this earth. As the vision unfolded, Esdras saw some wings disappear, other wings seemed to divide and give rise to additional wings, and finally even the heads disappeared until only the body of the eagle was left. After this dismal procession of the rise and fall of nations, Esdras saw a lion coming out of the forest.

> Then I heard a voice saying to me, "Look in front of you and consider what you see." When I looked, I saw what seemed to be a lion roused from the forest, roaring; and I heard how it uttered a human voice to the eagle, and spoke, saying, "Listen and I will speak to you. The Most High says to you, 'Are you not the one that remains of the four beasts that I made to reign in the world, so that the end of my times might come through them?'" (11:36-39)

As Esdras watched, he saw that "the whole body of the eagle was burned, and the earth was exceedingly terrified." (12:3) The angel gave Esdras the interpretation of the vision.

> And as for the lion whom you saw coming up out of the forest and roaring and speaking to the eagle and reproving him for his unrighteousness, and as for all the words that you have heard, this is the Messiah whom the Most High has kept until the end of the days, who will arise from the offspring of David, and will come and speak with them. He will denounce

> them for their ungodliness and their wickedness, and will display before them their contemptuous dealings. For first he will bring them alive before his judgment seat, and when he has reproved them, then he will destroy them. But in mercy he will set free the remnant of my people, those who have been saved throughout my borders, and he will make them joyful until the end comes, the Day of Judgment, of which I spoke to you at the beginning. (12:31-34)

For one who is familiar with the book of Revelation, the vision brings to mind the promise of Revelation 5:5: "He [that is Jesus] is the lion of the tribe of Judah, the root of David, who has triumphed." (NIV)

Vision Six

In vision six Esdras saw a man come up out of the sea, encounter lots of hostility, and later come down from a mountain to establish peace.

> After seven days I dreamed a dream in the night. And lo, a wind rose from the sea and stirred up all its waves. As I kept looking the wind made something like the figure of a man come up out of the heart of the sea. And I saw that this man flew with the clouds of heaven; and wherever he turned his face to look, everything under his gaze trembled, and whenever his voice issued from his mouth, all who heard his voice melted like wax when it feels the fire.

> After this I looked and saw that an innumerable number of people were gathered together from the four winds of heaven to make war against the man who came up out of the sea. (13:1-5)

So the man from the sea carved out for himself a mountain from which he breathed out fire and destruction on those who opposed him until nothing was left "but the dust of the earth and the smell of smoke." (13:11)

A bit later Esdras saw this same man gather another multitude, but this multitude was peaceful.

> After this I saw the same man come down from the mountain and call to himself another multitude that was peaceable. Then many people came to him, some of whom were joyful and some sorrowful; some of them were bound, and some were bringing others as offerings. (13:12-13)

Esdras reported that the vision terrified him, and he begged for an interpretation. The angel assumed the voice of God and explained the vision.

> This is the interpretation of the vision. As for your seeing a man come up from the heart of the sea, this is he whom the Most High has been keeping for many ages, who will himself deliver his creation; and he will direct those who are left. (13:25-26)

> The days are coming when the Most High will deliver those who are on the earth. (13:29)

> When these things take place and the signs occur that I showed you before, then my Son will be revealed, whom you saw coming up from the sea. (13:32)

> Then my Son will reprove the assembled nations for their ungodliness, and will reproach them to their face with their evil thoughts and the torments with which they are to be tormented and will destroy them. (13:37-38)

> But those who are left of your people, who ae found within my holy borders, shall be saved. Therefore when he destroys the multitude of the nations who are gathered together, he will defend the people who remain. And then he will show them very many wonders. (13:48-50)

Esdras said that he still did not understand it all. The angel responded,

> Just as no one can explore or know what is in the depths of the sea, so no one on earth can see my [God's] Son and those who are with him, except in the time of his day. (13:52)

Clearly the vision has to do with God's judgment on the wicked and his salvation for the righteous. But it is difficult to discern whether the vision is about the Babylonian captivity, the conquest by Rome, the incarnation, or the return of the Messiah in the final judgment; or perhaps all the above at different levels.

Vision Seven

The vision begins with God telling Esdras that he must get his house in order because he is going to be delivered from this present evil age and brought up to be with his Son. (14:9) The apocryphal Esdras, however, imagined the canonical Ezra's burden to give one last message of warning to the exiles in Babylon. Beyond that, he wanted to assure that generations to come would know what he knew. So he asked permission to stay alive until he could write it all down.

> Let me speak in your presence, Lord. For I will go, as you have commanded me, and I will reprove the people who are now living; but who will warn those who will be born hereafter? For the world lies in darkness, and the inhabitants are without light. For your law has been burned, and so no one knows the things which have been done or will be done by you. If then I have found favor with you, send your holy spirit into me, and I will write everything that has happened in the world from the beginning, the things that were written in your law, so that people may be able to find the path, and that those who want to live in the last days may do so. (14:19-22)

In this vision God gave Esdras permission. Furthermore God gave him five others to help him, promised his Holy Spirit to open their heats with understanding, and told him to take his five companions and go to a quiet place for forty days to accomplish the work. The result of their efforts was the writing of ninety-four books. And this is what God wanted Esdras to do with those books.

> And when the forty days were ended, the Most High spoke to me, saying, "Make public the twenty-four books that you wrote first, and let the worthy and the unworthy read them; but keep the seventy that were written last, in order to give them to the wise among your people. For in them is the spring of understanding, the fountain of wisdom, and the river of knowledge." And I did so. (14:45-48)

The twenty-four books correspond to the Hebrew canon where the thirty-nine books are reduced to twenty-four by combining Kings and Chronicles into single books, and by placing the twelve minor prophets into a single volume called "The Book of the Prophets." The seventy books that were not to be made public may well be a reference to the Gnosticism that was widespread in the first couple of centuries A.D. The Gnostics claimed to have secret knowledge of the mysteries of the faith. It was judged to be a heresy because Gnostic teachings went far beyond the accepted revelation of God.

Fourth Esdras concludes with an extensive address that the anonymous author imagined Ezra making to the exiles in Babylon. The address speaks of human sin, God's judgment, the deliverance of those who keep his commandments, and the need to be prepared for the day of the Lord.

The Goodspeed version of The Apocrypha (Vintage Books, New York, 1959) adds this postscript from the Greek at the end of the visions: "Then Ezra was caught up, and taken to the land of those who were like him, after he had written all this. And he was called the scribe of the knowledge of the Most High forever and ever." (pages 97, 98)

Things to Think About

At first glance it seems to be coldly insensitive when Esdras told the woman to stop weeping because all she lost was one son, whereas the whole world is dying in its sin. What do you think would be your reaction if a pastor told you at a time of grief that your sorrow was small compared to what should be our sorrow for the world? The church often prays for peace in the world, and for the salvation of those living in sin. How could the church express its sadness for those who are living in their sin – sometimes even within the church itself?

The apocryphal Esdras had a vision of an eagle and a lion. The prophet Daniel had a similar vision (chapter 7) of beasts and ultimate victory. Both visions tell of the march of the kingdoms of this earth through history, and the ultimate triumph of the kingdom of God. Does this visionary sketch of history give you comfort? Or fear? Or anxiety? Or hope? Explain.

In Esdras' vision the man who came up from the sea is the same as the man who came down from the mountain. Coming up from the sea he was in conflict with the powers of this world. Coming down from the mountain he was leader of a peaceable kingdom. In a Christian context, both "men" refer to Christ. What do you think: are we now living in the "man from the sea" times, or in the "man from the mountain" times? Is there any sense in which we can be living in both "times" at the same time?

The Apocryphal Books of History, Part One

Of the six books in this category only two of them record events that are not referenced in the canonical scripture. First and Second Maccabees chronicle the story of Israel during the four hundred years between the end of the Old Testament canon and the beginning of the New. The other four books in this category either summarize or add to the history that is told in the canonical books

Third Esdras

Like Fourth Esdras the author of this book adopted the name of canonical Ezra. It is likely that biblical Ezra wrote the Chronicles, Ezra, and Nehemiah. About 450 years later an anonymous Esdras wrote this book. Third Esdras is one of the three apocryphal books not accepted as authoritative by Roman Catholicism.

The book is largely a collection of pieces of historical information taken from the canonical books of First and Second Chronicles, Ezra, and Nehemiah. There is no chronological order to this material. It seems that Esdras was impressed by aspects of Israel's Babylonian captivity and wrote them down in random order. For the most part the material in Third Esdras is reasonably accurate to the canonical record. The significant exception is the imaginary account of the three guardsmen.

The three guardsmen apparently were Jewish exiles who had found favor with the Persian king, Darius. In fact, they were his personal body guards. Esdras imagined that one night the guardsmen hatched a plan, apparently with the king's endorsement. Each of the three guardsmen would write who or what he thought was the strongest.

> Then each wrote his own statement, and they sealed them and put them under the pillow of King Darius, and said, "When the King wakes, they will give him the writing and the one whose statement the king and the three nobles of Persia judge to be the wisest, the victory shall be given according to what is written."
>
> The first wrote, "Wine is strongest,."
>
> The second wrote, "The king is strongest."
>
> The third wrote, "Women are strongest, but above all things truth is victor." (3:8-12)

The next morning the king called his nobles and wise men together and demanded that each of the guardsmen defend his answer.

> The first, who had spoken of the strength of wine, began and said, "Gentlemen, how is wine

the strongest? It leads astray the minds of all who drink it. It makes equal the mind of the king and the orphan, of the slave and the free, of the poor and the rich. It turns every thought to feasting and mirth, and forgets all sorrow and debt." (3:17b-20)

The second, who had spoken of the strength of the king, began to speak. "Gentlemen, are not men strongest, who rule over land and sea, and all that is in them? But the king is stronger; he is their lord and master, and whatever he says to them they obey. If he tells them to make war on one another, they do it, and if he sends them out against the enemy, they go, and conquer mountains, walls, and towers." (4:2-4)

Then the third, who had spoken of women and truth, began to speak. "Gentlemen, is not the king great, and are not men many, and is not wine strong? Who is it, then, who rules them, or has the mastery over them? Is it not women? Women give birth to the king and to every people that rules over sea and land. From women they came; and women brought up the very men who plant the vineyards from which comes wine. Women make men's clothes; they bring men glory; men cannot exist without women. If men gather gold and silver or any other beautiful thing, and see a woman lovely in appearance and beauty, they let all those things go, and gape at her, and with open mouths stare at her, and prefer her to gold, silver, or any other beautiful thing." (4:13-19)

The king was not so impressed with the argument about women, but he did remember that this third guardsman had mentioned truth. King Darius said,

> Truth is great, and stronger than all things. The whole earth calls upon truth, and heaven blesses it. All God's works quake and tremble, and with him there is nothing unrighteous. Wine is unrighteous, the king is unrighteous, women are unrighteous, all human beings are unrighteous, all their works are unrighteous, and all such things. There is no truth in them and in their unrighteousness. They will perish. But truth endures and is strong forever." (4:35b-38)

And all the people shouted, "Great is truth and strongest of all." (4:41) As the king had promised, he offered the winning guardsman all kinds of riches and prestige. But the guardsman had his own request. He wanted nothing more than to go back to Jerusalem in order to restore the city.

A parenthetical statement in chapter 4:14 states that the name of the third guardsman was Zerubbabel. Although apocryphal Esdras does not make the connection, there are enough similarities to give rise to the tradition that Zerubbabel was really Nehemiah who gained permission to return to Jerusalem by winning the contest of the three guardsmen.

Canonical Nehemiah tells a different story. Nehemiah was cupbearer to Artaxerxes, king of Persia. He had heard of Jerusalem's sad state of disrepair and was deeply saddened because of it. One day the king noticed that Nehemiah was crestfallen, and asked him what would take away his sadness. Nehemiah responded: "If it pleases she king and if your servant has found favor in your sight, send me to the city of Jerusalem where my fathers are buried so that I can rebuild it." (Nehemiah 2:5 NIV) And that's how it happened.

Baruch

This book in the history collection was written by an anonymous author who imagined himself to be the canonical Baruch. Canonical Baruch was the prophet Jeremiah's secretary. (Jeremiah 45:1)

At the time of Jeremiah the Babylonians were systematically taking the residents of Judah and Jerusalem to Babylon. This tempted those who remained in Jerusalem to flee to Egypt for asylum. Jeremiah told the people that Judah must accept its Babylonian captivity as God's punishment for its sins and not run off to Egypt.

This offended those who wanted to escape. Apparently they blamed Baruch, claiming that he was persuading Jeremiah to tell them that it was God's will that they not flee to Egypt. Canonical Jeremiah records one such instance.

> And all the arrogant men said to Jeremiah, "You are lying! The Lord our God has not sent you to say, 'You must not go to Egypt to settle there.' But Baruch, son of Neriah, is inciting you against us to hand us over to the Babylonians so that they may kill us or carry us into exile in Babylon." (Jeremiah 43:2-3 NIV)

Apocryphal Baruch imagined Jeremiah's secretary in Babylon where he not only told the Jews not to flee to Egypt, but to remain where they were and there pray for and respect their captors. This is what he imagined to be the advice of Jeremiah and Baruch to Israel.

> Pray for the life of king Nebuchadnezzar of Babylon, and for the life of his son Belshazzar, so that their days on earth will be like the days of heaven. The Lord will give us strength, and light to our eyes; we shall live under the protection of King Nebuchadnezzar of Babylon and under the protection of his son Belshazzar and we shall serve them many days and find favor in their sight. (1:11-12)

The book continues with an extended prayer in which Baruch petitioned God for the forgiveness of Israel's sins. He reminded God of his promises to care for his people, and he pleaded for the day of deliverance from captivity. He ended with a confident message of hope.

> Take off the garment of your sorrow and affliction, O Jerusalem, and put on forever the beauty of the glory from God. Put on the robe of righteousness that comes from God; put on your head the diadem of the glory of the Everlasting, for God will show your splendor everywhere under heaven. For God will give you evermore the name "Righteous, Peace, Godly Glory." Arise. O Jerusalem, and stand on the height; and look toward the east, and see your children gathered from west and east at the word of

the Holy One, rejoicing that God has remembered them. (5:1-5)

The Letter of Jeremiah

The last chapter of Baruch is a letter that Baruch ascribed to Jeremiah. Some collections of the Apocrypha make chapter 6 of Baruch a separate book, entitled "The Letter of Jeremiah."

Canonical Jeremiah did write a letter to the exiles. It is recorded in Jeremiah 29. A comparison between the apocryphal letter and the canonical letter provides a fine example of a significant difference between the canonical books and the apocryphal books. In the canonical books God reveals himself and his will for his people. In the apocryphal books that divine revelation is muted, or it is missing altogether.

The apocryphal letter of Jeremiah begins with the word of Jeremiah reminding the people of their sins that brought them to Babylon. The letter continues with an extensive description of idols, and concludes with an observation about the folly of worshiping idol gods.

> Because of the sins that you have committed before God, you will be taken to Babylon as exiles by Nebuchadnezzar, king of the Babylonians. (Baruch 6:2; Letter of Jeremiah 1:2)

> Better, therefore, is someone upright who has no idols; such a person will be far above reproach. (Baruch 6:73; Letter of Jeremiah 1:73)

By contrast the letter of Jeremiah in the canonical book begins with God and is filled with evidences of divine compassion. The letter offers hope to the exiles in Babylon.

> "This is what the Lord Almighty, the God of Israel, says to those carried into exile." (Jeremiah 29:4 NIV)
>
> This is what the Lord says: "When seventy years are completed I will come to you and fulfill my gracious promise to bring you back to this place. For I know the plans I have for you," declares the Lord, "plan to prosper you and not harm you, plans to give you hope and a future. (Jeremiah 29:10-11 NIV)
>
> You will seek me and find me when you seek me with all your heart." (Jeremiah 29:13 NIV)

Addition to the Book of Esther

This apocryphal work is not really a separate book, but it is an addition to the book of Esther. A second century B.C. author apparently did not like the fact that the book of Esther shows very little Jewish piety, and does not even mention the name of God. So this anonymous author around 115 B.C. likely said to himself, "I can fix that." So he dressed out the book of Esther to make it sound more spiritual.

The book of Esther in most Protestant Bibles is the original version that was approved by the Council of Jamnia in 90 A.D. As early as the first century B.C the Septuagint, the Greek translation of the Old Testament, included the apocryphal additions as insertions into the flow of the original story.

The story is familiar. Judah was in its Babylonian captivity, now under Persian rule. King Xerxes had a feast at which Queen Vashti defied the king, so he banished her, and the Jewess Esther became queen in her place. The apocryphal author imagined a dream that Esther's cousin Mordecai might have had. He will explain the significance of his dream at the end of the book.

> And this was his dream: noises and confusion, thunders and earthquake, tumult on the earth. Then two great dragons came forward, both ready to fight, and they roared terribly. At their roaring every nation prepared for war, to fight against the righteous nation. It was a day of darkness and gloom, tribulation and distress, affliction and great tumult on the earth. And the whole righteous nation was troubled; they feared the evils that threatened them, and were ready to perish. Then they cried out to God, and at their outcry, as though from a tiny spring, there came a great river, with abundant water. Light came, and the sun arose, and the lowly were exalted and devoured those held in honor. (Addition A, 11:5-11)

The story continues. Under the influence of evil Haman the Jews were threatened with national extinction. Mordecai challenged Esther to appeal to the king for the Jewish people. Canonical Esther reports that Esther fasted before she went in to the king. The apocryphal author imagined a prayer that Esther may have offered while she was fasting.

> O my Lord, You only are our King, help me, who am alone and have no helper but you, for my danger is in my hand. Ever since I was born I have heard in the tribe of my family that you, O Lord, took Israel out of all the nations, and all our ancestors from among all their forebears for an everlasting inheritance, and that you did for them all that you promised. And now we have sinned before you, and you have handed us over to our enemies because we glorified their gods. You are righteous, O Lord! And now they are not satisfied that we are in bitter slavery, but they have covenanted with their idols to abolish what your mouth has ordained, to destroy your inheritance, to stop the mouths of those who praise you and to quench your altar and the glory of your house, to open the mouths of the nations for the praise of vain idols, and to magnify forever a mortal king. O Lord, do not surrender your scepter to what has no being, and do not let them laugh at our downfall, but turn their plan against them, and make an example of him who began this against us. (Addition C - 14:3-11)

Israel was spared. Evil Haman was hanged on the gallows that he had prepared for Mordecai. And Mordecai explained the dream that he had at the beginning of the story.

> And Mordecai said, "These things have come from God; for I remember the dream that I had concerning these matters, and none of them has failed to be fulfilled. There was the little spring

that became a river, and there was light and sun and abundant water – the river is Esther, whom the king married and made queen. The two dragons are Haman and myself. The nations are those that gathered to destroy the name of the Jews. And my nation, this is Israel who cried out to God and was saved. The Lord has saved his people, the Lord has rescued us from all these evils, God has done great signs and wonders, wonders that have never happened among the nations." (Addition F :4-9)

It might have been nice if these expressions of piety had been part of the original story of Esther that nurtured the faith of Israel. But the fact is that these additions were made centuries later.

The Prayer of Manasseh

The Prayer of Manasseh is the shortest of apocryphal books. It has a place in the apocryphal books of history because the anonymous author imagined a prayer that the historical Manasseh might have offered after he turned to the Lord.

Manasseh was the wicked son of a godly father. His father was King Hezekiah, of whom we read in II Kings 18:3, "He did what was right in the eyes of the Lord." (NIV) Manasseh was twelve years old when he became king. He ruled for thirty years leading Israel into idolatry, prostitution, and child sacrifice. He was so evil that II Kings 21:16 reports, "Manasseh also shed so much innocent blood that he filled Jerusalem from end to end." (NIV) God punished him by bringing him into captivity in Assyria. It was there that he met his

Master face to face. II Chronicles 33:12-13 reports that he humbled himself greatly and he prayed to the Lord.

Hundreds of years later an anonymous author wrote a prayer that he imagined a penitent Manasseh offered to God. All those who have pleaded with God for forgiveness after a record of sin could easily make Manasseh's prayer their own. In the first part of his prayer Manasseh praised God for his greatness and for the greatness of his mercy. Then he opened his heart in guilt before the Lord.

> The sins I have committed are more in number than the sand of the seas; my transgressions are multiplied. O Lord, they are multiplied! I am not worthy to look up and see the height of heaven because of the multitude of my iniquities. I am weighed down with many an iron fetter, so that I am rejected because of my sins, and I have no relief, for I have provoked your wrath, and have done what is evil in your sight, setting up abominations and multiplying offenses.
>
> And now I bend the knee of my heart, imploring you for your kindness. I have sinned, O Lord, I have sinned, and I acknowledge my transgressions. I earnestly implore you, forgive me, O Lord, forgive me! Do not destroy me with my transgressions! Do not be angry with me forever or store up evil for me; do not condemn me to the depths of the earth. For you, O Lord, are the God of those who repent, and in me you will manifest your goodness; for, unworthy as I am, you will save me according to your great mercy, and I will praise you continually

all the days of my life. For all the host of heaven sings your praise, and yours is the glory forever. Amen (verses 9-15)

The prayer is a jewel among the apocryphal writings. One could hope that Manasseh offered that kind of prayer. Maybe he did. But the prayer was not written until hundreds of years after the time of Manasseh, and there is no indication in II Chronicles of such a prayer.

This apocryphal book is not accepted as canonical by Roman Catholicism, perhaps because there is no indication of a confessional, an intermediary, or penance. Manasseh appealed directly and unconditionally to God for mercy and forgiveness.

Things to think about

Apocryphal Baruch said that the Jews should stay in their captivity. They should not resist the Babylonians, but pray for them and respect them, leading peaceful lives in exile. Read Matthew 5:44 and Romans 13:1-7. Are there any limits to this? Or exceptions?

The book of Esther makes no mention of God. Yet apparently it was accepted without challenge at the Council of Jamnia in 90 A.D. as part of God's inspired revelation. Does God reveal himself in Esther? And if so, how, and what does he say about himself? How does God reveal himself today?

Manasseh prayed for forgiveness. Does God always forgive our sins when we ask him to? What about "fruits of repentance"? Why is it that sometimes we pray for forgiveness, but we don't feel forgiven? What does it mean to "forgive ourselves"?

THE APOCRYPHAL BOOKS OF HISTORY, PART TWO

The Maccabees

The two books of Maccabees are perhaps the most familiar of the Old Testament Apocrypha. They are a valuable resource dealing with the history of Israel during the 400 years between Malachi and the birth of John the Baptist. They were put in the list of Apocrypha because, although they are good history, there is no evidence of divine revelation. There is no record of divinely appointed prophets at work during this period, as was the case in the canonical books that record the history of Israel.

When the Old Testament came to an end Persia was the major power of the day. Under the Persians the Jews were permitted to go back to Judea and rebuild Jerusalem and its temple, but they still remained under Persian rule. Shortly before 330 B.C. Alexander the Great and his armies conquered Palestine and its neighbors, placing the entire region under Grecian rule. Grecian influence developed rapidly, but Grecian rule was short lived. About 12 years after his conquest of Persia Alexander got sick and died while trying to establish a capital city in Babylon.

First Maccabees 1:5-6 tells us that before his death Alexander divided his empire among his most honored officers who then succeeded him. An officer named Seleucus was given what we know as the Middle East, which included Palestine. Seleucus made Antioch of Syria his capital city, thus establishing Antiochus as the ruling family's name and Syria as the name of the region that Alexander the Great had assigned to him.

Seleucus, who was now known as Antiochus the First, began his rule shortly after 300 B.C. He and the several who succeeded him did not pay a whole lot of attention to Palestine because they were involved in conflicts with Egypt. After about 100 years the succession of Antiochan rulers led to Antiochus the Fourth. He was also known as Antiochus Epiphanes.

Antiochus Epiphanes was determined to force all people under his rule into the mold of Greek culture and Grecian religious practices. Anything non-Greek was forbidden. That was no special problem for countries with no strong religious tradition. It simply meant that people had to transfer their worship of Persian gods to Greek gods. But to faithful Jews the requirement of Epiphanes was an enormous problem. In order to become practicing Greek Gentiles the Jews had to abandon the whole structure of festivals, sacrifices, and ordinances that were commanded in the law and the prophets. Jewish rebellion against Antiochus Epiphanes is the story told in First and Second Maccabees.

What is known as the Maccabean Period began in 175 B.C. with Jewish resistance to the decrees of Antiochus Epiphanes. The Period ended around 135 B.C. under the leadership of the high priest Simon. The Maccabean War between Syria and Israel ran from 167 to 160 B.C.

Although the authorship of First and Second Maccabees is not known, the style of writing suggests that the books were written by two different authors during or shortly after the Maccabean period.

The anonymous authors were probably eye witness Jews living in Palestine.

First Maccabees

First Maccabees opens with the report of Alexander the Great's death and the rise of the Antiochus family. Chapter 1:10 reports: "From them [that is, the Antiochus family] came forth a sinful root, Antiochus Epiphanies."

Antiochus Epiphanes was profane and cruel. It is difficult to comprehend the horror that he visited on faithful Jews who refused to adopt the ways of the Gentiles. In the interest of establishing Greek culture Epiphanies outlawed circumcision, Sabbath observance, religious festivals, and as the ultimate insult to Jewish religious practices he sacrificed a pig on the altar in the temple in Jerusalem. Chapter one opens just a window into the horrors that the righteous Jews endured.

> The king sent letters by messengers to Jerusalem and the towns of Judah; he directed them to follow customs strange to the land, to forbid burnt offerings and sacrifices and drink offerings in the sanctuary, to profane the Sabbaths and festivals, to defile the sanctuary and the priests, to build altars and sacred precincts and shrines for idols to sacrifice swine and other unclean animals, and to have their sons uncircumcised. They were to make themselves abominable by everything unclean and profane, so that they would forget the law and change all the

ordinances. He added, "And whoever does not obey the command of the king shall die." (1:44-50)

According to the decrees they put to death the women who had their children circumcised and their families and those who circumcised them; and they hung the infants from their mother's necks. (1:60-61)

Under that pressure a number of Jews abandoned their faith and followed the rules of Antiochus. But in Palestine there was a faithful Jew whose name was Mattathias. He had five sons. Mattathias gave expression to the grief of his family over the terrible decrees of Antiochus Epiphanes.

[Mattathias] saw the blasphemies being committed in Judah and Jerusalem, and he said, "Alas! Why was I born to see this, the ruin of my people, the ruin on the holy city, and to live there when it was given over to the enemy, the sanctuary given over to aliens? Her temple has become like a person without honor; her glorious vessels have been carried into exile. Her infants have been killed in her streets, her youths by the sword of the foe." (2:6-9)

Then Mattathias and his sons tore their clothes, put on sackcloth, and mourned greatly. (2:14)

Mattathias and his sons began a campaign that, at first, was directed against those Jews who had abandoned the faith to obey the decrees of Epiphanes.

> [Mattathias and his sons] organized an army, and struck down sinners in their anger and renegades in their wrath; Mattathias and his friends went around and tore down the altars; they forcibly circumcised all the uncircumcised boys they found within the borders of Israel. They hunted down the arrogant, and the work prospered in their hands. They rescued the law out of the hands of the Gentiles and kings, and they never let the sinner gain the upper hand. (2:44-48)

When Mattathias knew that his death was imminent, he gathered his sons around him, and gave them their instructions for leading the Jews in resisting the decrees of Antiochus Epiphanes.

> Now the days drew near for Mattathias to die, and he said to his sons, "Arrogance and storm have now become strong; it is a time of ruin and furious anger. Now, my children, show zeal for the law, and give your lives for the covenant of our ancestors. (2:49-50)

> Judas Maccabeus has been a mighty warrior from his youth. He shall command the army for you and fight the battle against the peoples. You shall rally around you all who observe the law, and avenge the wrong done to your people. Pay back the Gentiles in full, and obey the demands of the law." Then he blessed them and was gathered to his ancestors. (2:66-69)

Initially Judas continued the campaign of his father against the unfaithful Jews. But the conflict soon escalated into war between the Syrians under Antiochus Epiphanes and the Israelites under Judas Maccabeus. When Antiochus was told of this Maccabean opposition to his decrees he sent his general Lysias to destroy the forces of Judas and all those who supported the Maccabean uprising. In one of the great battles of the war the Maccabeans defeated Lysias, marched victoriously into Jerusalem, cleansed the temple, repaired the altars, and celebrated their great victory with an eight day feast that faithful Jews still celebrate today, known as Hanukah, an eight day festival of lights each December.

> So they celebrated the dedication of the altar for eight days, and joyfully offered burnt offerings; they offered a sacrifice of well-being and a thanksgiving offering. They decorated the front of the temple with golden crowns and small shields; they restored the gates and the chambers for the priests, and fitted them with doors. There was very great joy among the people, and the disgrace brought by the Gentiles was removed. Then Judas and his brothers and all the assembly of Israel determined that every year at that season the days of dedication of the altar should be observed with joy and gladness for eight days. (4:56-59)

When Epiphanes heard about the defeat of Lysias and the rededication of the temple in Jerusalem, he "became sick from disappointment" and in 163 B.C. he died. (6:8-16) He was succeeded by his son Eupator.

The war continued on a variety of fronts with Judas and the Maccabean army determined to preserve historic Judaism, and the Syrian army determined to crush the Jewish resistance movement. In the last battle of Judas Maccabeus an army of twenty-two thousand Syrians was arrayed against Judas and eight hundred of his faithful warriors (9:4, 6). In that battle of 160 B.C. Judas was killed. First Maccabees records Israel's grief over the loss of their hero.

> All Israel made great lamentation for him; they mourned many days and said, "How is the mighty fallen, the savior of Israel!" (9:20-21)

The brothers of Judas, Jonathan and Simon, took over leadership of the Jewish resistance. Although skirmishes continued, there was no great final victory for the Maccabees, nor was there an unconditional surrender by the Syrians. The decrees of Epiphanes were still on the books, but they were not universally enforced. Syria had to accept the fact that they could not defeat the Maccabees either by decree or by war. First Maccabees reports:

> Thus the sword ceased from Israel. Jonathan ruled in Michmash and began to judge the people, and he destroyed the godless out of Israel. (9:73)

For the next several chapters First Maccabees chronicles the post war period in Palestine. It was a time of political intrigue, military treachery, occasional up-risings, conflict with Egypt, and an alliance with Rome. On one occasion Syrian forces captured Jonathan and killed him (12:48). His brother Simon assumed leadership in his place.

Simon was the leader under whose administration the Jews finally gained their economic and religious independence. In response to a letter from Simon, Syrian king Antiochus Demetrius pardoned "the errors and offenses [that the Jews] had committed to this day." (13:39) First Maccabees reports:

> [In 142 B.C.] the yoke of the Gentiles was removed from Israel and the people began to write in their documents and contracts, "In the first year of Simon the great high priest and commandeer and leader of the Jews."(13:41-42)

Under Simon the Jews enjoyed a time of relative peace. Unfortunately, Simon was not able to continue his leadership of the Jews because in 134 B.C. he and two of his sins were assassinated in an act of Syrian treachery. His son John succeeded him. Alliances with Rome gave the Jews added security. In the middle of the first century B.C. Judea became a Roman province. The history of Israel continues in the New Testament and the Herods.

Second Maccabees

Second Maccabees was written by an anonymous Jew who called himself "the compiler." (2:28) He claimed that his work summarized five other volumes that chronicled the Maccabean Period. He recalled several events that are also told in First Maccabees, but not always in the same order. At times it seems that he was more interested in highlighting dramatic events than in providing a chronology of the Maccabean Period.

The book has an interesting structure. The author began with a "Preface" in which he told us what he planned to do, and it ended with an "Epilogue" in which he apologized for any inadequacies.

The Preface

The story of Judas Maccabeus and his brothers, and the purification of the great temple, and the dedication of the altar, and further the wars against Antiochus Epiphanes and his son Eupator, and the appearances that came from heaven to those who fought bravely for Judaism, so that though few in number they seized the whole land and punished the barbarian hordes, and regained possession of the temple famous throughout the world, and liberated the city, and established the laws that were about to be abolished, while the Lord with great kindness became glorious to them – all this, which has been set forth by Jason of Cyrene in five volumes, we shall attempt to condense into a single book. (2:19-23)

The Epilogue

So I will here end my story. If it has been well told and to the point, that is what I myself desired; if it was poorly done and mediocre, that was the best I could do. (15:38)

Between the preface and the epilogue the author focused especially on the heroism of Judas Maccabeus. First Maccabees tells the history; Second Maccabees honors the hero. It would be comparable to someone writing the history of the American Revolutionary War, and then another author writing a book to honor George Washington's role in that war.

Chapters three to five repeat the report in First Maccabees of the growing apostasy of many Jews. This emboldened Antiochus Epiphanes to such arrogance that, states chapter 5:21, "he thought "that he could sail on the land and walk on the sea." In his arrogance he pressed his decrees on all the Jews.

> Harsh and utterly grievous was the onslaught of evil. For the temple was filled with debauchery and reveling by the Gentiles, who dallied with prostitutes and had intercourse with women within the sacred precincts, and besides brought in things for sacrifice that were unfit. The altar was covered with abominable offerings that were forbidden by the laws. People could not keep the Sabbath, nor observe the festivals of their ancestors, nor so much as confess themselves to be Jews. (6:3-6)

That was the abomination that motivated Judas Maccabeus and his brothers to gather an army to call the Jews back to covenant faithfulness and to resist the terrible decrees of Epiphanes. The rest of Second Maccabees honors the exploits of Judas. Two events are particularly interesting. In the first, Judas returned to Jerusalem after one of his victorious battles.

> Therefore, carrying ivy-wreathed wands and beautiful branches and also fronds of palm, they offered hymns of thanksgiving to him who had given success to the purifying of his own holy place. (10:7)

That parade in honor of Judas Maccabeus reminds us of that story in New Testament history about the triumphal entrance of Jesus into Jerusalem on Palm Sunday (Matthew 21:1-11). It was the second century B.C. version of today's ticker-tape parade.

The second passage that deserves attention records the plan of Judas to make atonement for those who had died.

> He [Judas Maccabeus] also took up a collection, man by man, to the amount of two thousand drachmas of silver, and sent it to Jerusalem to provide for a sin offering. In doing this he acted very well and honorably, taking account of the resurrection. For if he were not expecting that those who had fallen would rise again, it would have been superfluous and foolish to pray for the dead. But if he was looking to the splendid reward that is laid up for those who fall asleep in godliness, it was a holy and pious thought. Therefore he made atonement for the dead, so that they might be delivered from their sin. (12:43-45)

This passage makes interesting reading because it relates to Roman Catholic doctrines of prayers for the dead, penance, and purgatory. For good reason the Council of Trent in 1546 approved Second Maccabees as authoritative for the church.

Near the end of the book the anonymous author praised God. He wrote, "Blessed is he who has kept his own place [the temple] undefiled." (15:34)

Things to Think About

The Jews faced enormous opposition and incredible cruelty. Faithful Jews went to war against unfaithful Jews as well as against the military and political powers that were trying to eliminate all evidences of piety. What do you think you would do under similar circumstances today?

The temple was the "church" for the Jews. When the temple was defiled the Jews went to war. What would you do if your church was spray painted with satanic symbols, or a goat was sacrificed to the devil in the church's parking lot? Would you prosecute?

It was clear that the forces of Antiochus Epiphanes were the enemy to Judas Maccabeus and his brothers. It may be less clear that the unfaithful Jews were the enemy. Who are the enemies of the Christian faith today? Where are those enemies? How should Christians deal with them?

THE APOCRYPHAL BOOKS OF WISDOM, PART ONE

Wisdom Literature

The phrase "wisdom literature" identifies a category of biblical books. The most familiar kinds of literature in the Old Testament are "the books of law," and "the books of the prophets." But the category of wisdom was also recognized in Israel. Jeremiah 18:18 refers to the reading of the law by the priests, the counsel of the wise, and the word from the prophets. The wisdom books of the Old Testament are Job, Proverbs, and Ecclesiastes, along with a few of the Psalms.

Biblical wisdom literature is not law, nor prophetic utterance, nor logical argument. It rather invites us to a pious reflection on what it means to live as God's people in God's world. At times wisdom literature teaches by exploring a problem such as suffering in the book of Job. Or it may reflect on the quality and character of life as does the book of Ecclesiastes. Or wisdom literature may consist of maxims, sayings, guidelines for living wisely as does the book of Proverbs.

Underlying biblical wisdom is the conviction that this world and all that is in it belongs to God. He created it. He governs it. The only way to live harmoniously is to live within God's order, as his image bearers in his world. Folly is to ignore God, resulting in a life of vanity and ultimate futility, out of sorts with the way God intended life to be. Wisdom is to "acknowledge God in all our ways" (Proverbs 3:6) resulting in a life of purpose, blessing, and hope. That is why biblical wisdom grounds its teaching in God. "The fear of the Lord is the beginning of wisdom." (Proverbs 1:7) "Remember your Creator in the days of your youth." (Ecclesiastes 12:1) And the only answer that God gave to Job's problem of suffering was a recitation of his sovereign power.

The fourteen book apocryphal collection includes two books in the wisdom category. These books say many of the same things that we find in canonical wisdom. They were designated as apocryphal, not because of their content, but because they were part of a body of Greek literature written centuries after Job, Proverbs, and Ecclesiastes had been accepted by Israel as authoritative Hebrew Scriptures.

Jesus Sirach, also known as Ecclesiasticus

This is the only book of the Apocrypha in which we know the author. He gives us his name and lineage in the opening chapter. His name in the Greek was "Jesus," and he was the son of "Sirach," therefore, "Jesus ben Sirach." In the third century after Christ the book was also named Ecclesiasticus, which translates into "the book of the church." It was likely so named because of its practical guidelines into interpersonal relationships that are so vital to living in community with God and his people.

Jesus ben Sirach was an orthodox Jew, living in Palestine, who wrote his book of wisdom around 175 B.C. Although most Old Testament Apocrypha were written in the Greek language, Jesus Sirach wrote this book in Hebrew. The prologue tells us that his grandson, who was living in Egypt, translated his grandpa's book into Greek. This was the copy that was available to Jerome when he translated the Scriptures into Latin.

The book is significant because it shows that living wisely meant essentially the same thing in the days of Sirach in 175 B.C. as it did at the time of Solomon back in 900 B.C. For Solomon, for Sirach, and still for us today biblical wisdom begins in "the fear of the Lord."

> The fear of the Lord delights the heart, gives gladness and joy and long life. Those who fear the Lord will have a happy end; on the day of their death they will be blessed. To fear the Lord is the beginning of wisdom. (1:12-14)

On that foundation the author proceeded for forty three of the fifty one chapters to offer guidelines on a wide variety of aspects of practical living. There is no special order. In fact he often provides us with a snippet of wisdom and several chapters later will return to the same issue with essentially the same advice. Reading the book is like reading someone's stream of consciousness. What follows is a sampling of Jesus Sirach's understanding of what it means to live within the fear of the Lord.

Guidelines about children

> My child, help your father in his old age, and do not grieve him as long as he lives, even if his mind fails, be patient with him, because you have all your faculties do not despise him. For kindness to a father will not be forgotten, and will be credited to you against your sins. (3:12-14)

Guidelines about friends

> When you gain friends, gain them through testing, and do not trust them instantly. For there are friends who are such when it suits them, but they will not stand by you in time of trouble. And there are friends who change into enemies, and tell of the quarrel to your disgrace. And there are friends who sit at your table, but they will not stand by you in time of trouble. When you are prosperous, they become your second self, and lord it over your servants; but if you are brought low, they turn against you, and hide themselves from you. (6:7-12)

> Do not abandon old friends, for new ones cannot equal them. A new friend is like new wine; when it has aged, you can drink it with pleasure. (9:10)

Guidelines about lust

> Do not give yourself to a woman and let her trample down your strength. Do not go near a loose woman, or you will fall into her snares. Do not dally with a singing girl, or you will be caught by her tricks. Do not look intently at a woman or you may stumble and incur penalties for her. Do not give yourself to prostitutes, or you may lose your inheritance. (9:2-6)

Guidelines about humility

> The wisdom of the humble lifts their heads high, and seats them among the great. Do not praise individuals for their good looks, or loathe anyone because of appearance alone. The bee is small among flying creatures, but what it produces is the best of sweet things. (11:1-3)

Guidelines about marriage

> Drooping hands and weak knees come from a wife who does not make her husband happy. From a woman sin had its beginning, and because of her we all die. Allow no outlet to water, and no boldness to an evil wife. If she does not go as you direct, therefore separate her from yourself. (25:23b-26)

> Happy is the husband who has a good wife; the number of his days will be doubled. A loyal wife brings joy to her husband, and he will complete his years in peace. A good wife is a great blessing, she will be granted among the blessings of the man who fears the Lord. (26:1-3)

Guidelines about table manners

> Eat what is set before you like a well brought-up person, and do not chew greedily or you will give offense. (31:16)

About half way through the book the author gave us a summary insight into what he understood by wisdom and folly.

> I take pleasure in three things, and they are beautiful in the sight of God and of mortals: agreement among brothers and sisters, friendship among neighbors, and a wife and a husband who live in harmony. I hate three kinds of people, and I loathe their manner of life: a pauper who boasts, a rich man who lies, and an old fool who commits adultery. (25:1-2)

Most of the sayings of Jesus ben Sirach are practical implications of Jesus' summary of the second table of the law: "Love your neighbor as yourself." (Matthew 22:39 NIV) Wisdom is to love and respect one another. Folly is to love and have regard only for self.

In chapter forty four Sirach did what the author of the Letter to the Hebrews did in chapter eleven. Hebrews eleven records some of the heroes of faith. Ecclesiasticus forty four begins a recital of more than a dozen of the heroes of wisdom. Jesus Sirach began the section with a statement that has often been quoted: "Let us now praise famous men." (44:1) Among Sirach's famous men were Enoch, Moses, the Judges, Elijah, Hezekiah, and others. Sirach honored these heroes because he found them to be good examples of what it meant to him to live wisely under the fear of the Lord

The apocryphal author concluded the book with a prayer of thanks to God for his salvation, and for helping him in the face of trouble.

> I cried out, "Lord, you are my Father, do not forsake me in the days of trouble, when there is

no help against the proud. I will praise your name continually, and sing hymns of thanksgiving for you have saved me from destruction, and delivered me in the time of trouble. For this reason I thank and praise you, and I bless the name of the Lord." (51:10-12)

In addition to his remarkably comprehensive description of what it means to live wisely as God's people in God's world Jesus Sirach's "Wisdom" has three qualities that deserve special mention.

First, Sirach occasionally interrupts his guidelines to bring praise to God. For Jesus Sirach God is the One of infinite glory and matchless power whose greatness is unsearchable, and whose creative skill is beyond understanding.

> Who can measure his majestic power? And who can fully recount his mercies? (18:5)

> When the Lord created his works from the beginning, and, in making them, determined their boundaries, he arranged his works in an eternal order, and their dominion for all generations. (16:26-27a)

A second feature deserving of special attention is the way in which Sirach often paused to pray. Prayer is not a prominent feature in the canonical books of wisdom. But Jesus ben Sirach brought to God his prayers of praise, petition, and confession.

> Have mercy upon us, O God of all, and put the nations in fear of you. Lift up our hand against

foreign nations and let them see your might. As you have used us to show your holiness to them, so use them to show your glory to us. Then they will know, as we have known, that there is no God but you, O Lord. (36:1-5)

A third feature worth noting is the way in which Jesus Sirach handled one of the Bible's familiar paradoxes, Are the affairs of life and our ultimate salvation determined by the sovereign God (divine election)? Or does the way we live and whether we are saved depend on our personal decision (free will)? Sirach said, "yes." Both statements are true, and Sirach was wise enough not to try to reconcile them.

On the one hand, he wrote that it's all up to God.

> All human beings come from the ground, and humankind was created out of dust. In the fullness of his knowledge the Lord distinguished them and appointed their different ways. Some he blessed and exalted, and some he made holy and brought near to himself, but some he cursed and brought low, and turned them out of their place. Like clay in the hand of the potter, to be molded as he pleased, so all are in the hand of their Maker, to be given whatever he decides. (33:10-13)

On the other hand Sirach wrote that it is all up to us.

> It was he [God] who created humankind in the beginning, and he left them in the power of their own free choice. If you choose, you can keep the

commandments, and to act faithfully is a matter of your own choice. He has placed before you fire and water, stretch out your hand for whichever you choose. Before each person are life and death; and whichever one chooses will be given. (15:14-17)

Thinks to Think About

Read Philippians 2:12-13. What does this passage seem to say about Jesus Sirach's paradox regarding divine election and free will?

What does it mean to "fear the Lord?" Is there ever any sense in which we ought to be afraid of God?

What is the difference between wisdom and self-control? Is it possible to be wise and not self-disciplined? Is it possible to be self-disciplined and not wise?

Read the Letter of James, chapter 1:5-8. What does this passage say about the character of wisdom and how to get it? Have you ever tried what James seems to promise? Did it accomplish results?

The Apocryphal Books of Wisdom, Part Two

The Wisdom of Solomon

The "Wisdom of Solomon" is also known as "The Book of Wisdom," or simply as "Wisdom." Late intertestamental Judaism and early Christianity speculated whether this book was originally written by Solomon. In chapters eight and nine the words and prayer are actually ascribed to Solomon, son of King David.

> I loved her [wisdom] and sought her from my youth; I desired to take her for my bride, and became enamored of her beauty. She glorifies her noble birth by living with God, and the Lord of all loves her. She is an initiate in the knowledge of God, and an associate in his works. (8:2-4)

Closer study, however, made clear that it could not have been written by David's son, for two reasons.

First, this apocryphal book in its original form was written in the Greek language. Although the Greek language dates back before the time of Solomon, the language was not exported to Palestine until the conquests of Alexander the Great around 330 B.C. So it is highly unlikely that King Solomon had any knowledge of Greek, and therefore could not have written this book. And even if, in a miracle of inspiration God would have enabled Solomon to know Greek well enough to write this book, the people of his day would not have been able to read it.

The second reason for which Solomon could not have written this Book of Wisdom lies in the way in which wisdom is presented. For Solomon, and also for Jesus Sirach, wisdom was essentially a virtue. It was a quality that is both expressed and nurtured through responsible living according to God's order of creation. In the Hebrew mind, wisdom was an "it."

By contrast and under the growing influence of Greek thinking wisdom was a "she" for the author of The Book of Wisdom. Wisdom was personified. Wisdom can think. It has emotions. It seems that in the mind of the author wisdom is a person who is to be known, loved, and followed. To be wise is not simply following the guidelines to responsible living, but to be wise is to be in some form of personal relationship with the divine.

Perhaps the best way to illustrate this Greek style of thinking is to use the language of the Apostle Paul. In I Corinthians 1:24 and 30, and again in Colossians 2:3 Paul wrote that Christ is the wisdom of God, he is the wisdom who came from God, and all God's wisdom is in him. If we want to be wise, Paul was saying, we have to begin with Christ. Grasp him by faith. Commit yourself to him. Living wisely is to know him and follow him. Living foolishly is to ignore Christ who is the very wisdom of God.

The anonymous author of The Book of Wisdom did not know Christ, nor could he have been familiar with the doctrine of the Trinity. Yet at times he seems to say that wisdom is God, yet it also sits next to God, or is sent from God, or is the Spirit of God. By wisdom the world was created, and therefore wisdom is before all things. So it is not surprising that the opening chapters of The Book of Wisdom provide us with a cosmic picture of where it all begins: with the Creator God who presides over a humanity that was made good, but is now broken by sin.

> For God created us for incorruption, and made us in the image of his own eternity. But through the devil's envy death entered the world, and those who belong to his company experience it. (2:23-24)

The apocryphal author surveyed the world and found some who are living in harmony with wisdom. They are the righteous. Their end will be blessedness. But so many others are living out of harmony with wisdom. They are the unrighteous. Unless they turn their hearts to wisdom, their end will be destruction. A pair of readings illustrate the careless abandon of the unrighteous and the bitter after-taste of a life of sin.

In the first reading, the author imagined himself to be in the company of the wicked as they describe the joys of living an unbridled life of sin.

> Come, therefore, let us enjoy the good things that exist and make use of the creation to the full as in youth. Let us take our fill of costly wine and perfumes, and let no flower of spring pass us by. Let us crown ourselves with rosebuds before they whither. Let none of us fail to share in our revelry; everywhere let us leave signs of enjoyment, because this is our portion, and this is our lot. Let us oppress

> the righteous poor man; let us not spare the widow or regard the gray hairs of the aged. (2:6-10)

In the second of this pair of readings the author again imagined himself to be in the company of the unrighteous who have now discovered the futility of their life without the restraint of wisdom.

> We took our fill of the paths of lawlessness and destruction, and we journeyed through trackless deserts, but the way of the Lord we have not known. What has our arrogance profited us? And what good has our boasted wealth brought us? All those things have vanished like a shadow, and like a rumor that passes by, like a ship that sails through billowy water, and when it has passed, no trace can be found, no track of its keel in the waves. (5:7-10)

In contrast to the apparent carefree life of the unrighteous the righteous may appear to be plagued with difficulties, but their troubles are in the hand of God who is shaping them into vessels fit for eternal blessedness.

> Having been disciplined a little, they will receive great good, because God tested them and found them worthy of himself; like gold in the furnace he tried them, and like a sacrificial burnt offering he accepted them. (3:5-6)

At the end the righteous and the unrighteous will all fall under the judgment of the eternal God. In various ways the author pictures the unrighteous on that final Day of Judgment.

> The Lord will laugh them to scorn. After this they will become dishonored corpses, and an outrage among the dead forever; because he will dash them speechless to the ground, and shake them to the foundations; they will be left utterly dry and barren, and they will suffer anguish, and the memory of them will perish. (4:18b-19)

In contrast to the destruction of the wicked, the author pictured the blessedness of the righteous.

> But the righteous live forever, and their reward is with the Lord; the Most High takes care of them. Therefore they will receive a glorious crown and a beautiful diadem from the hand of the Lord, because with his right hand he will cover them; and with his arm he will shield them. (5:15-16)

In this book of nineteen chapters, the first five chapters are devoted to that comprehensive description of the world populated both by the righteous and the unrighteous. All people are accountable to the God who created them, who preserves them, and who will one day judge them. After laying that foundation, the author turned his attention to wisdom.

> There is in her [wisdom] a spirit that is intelligent, holy, unique, manifold, subtle, mobile, clear, unpolluted, distinct, invulnerable, loving the good, keen, irresistible, beneficent, humane, steadfast, sure, free from anxiety, all-powerful, overseeing all, and penetrating through all spirits that are

> intelligent, pure, and altogether subtle. For wisdom is more mobile than any motion; because of her pureness pervades and penetrates all things. For she is the breath of the power of God, and a pure emanation of the glory of the Almighty; therefore nothing defiled can gain entrance into her. For she is a reflection of eternal light, a spotless mirror of the working of God, and an image of his goodness. (7:22-26)

Clearly, it is impossible for the author to think about wisdom without thinking about God. At one point he offers a prayer in which he thinks of wisdom sitting on a throne next to God.

> O God of my ancestors and Lord of mercy, who have made all things by your word; and by your wisdom have formed humankind to have dominion over the creatures you have made, and rule the world in holiness and righteousness, and pronounce judgment in uprightness of soul, give me the wisdom that sits by your throne. (9:1-4)

So what is wisdom to the unknown author of this book? Is it God himself? Or does it come from God? In a New Testament context might we say that wisdom is Christ? Or the Holy Spirit? At any rate, in some sense God and wisdom are inseparable. We gain wisdom to the degree that we draw our wisdom from him who is wisdom. To paraphrase the language of Paul: "For me to live wisely is Christ; for in him I live, and move, and have my being." (Philippians 1:21; Acts 17:28 NIV)

About half way through the book the material changes. The author drew from the history of Israel to warn his fellow Israelites about the folly of idol worship and the value of worshiping the God of his ancestors. An interesting and subtle shift occurs about half way through this section. When the section begins in chapter eleven the subject of the sentence is "wisdom." When the section ends the subject of the sentence is "God" as if there is no difference between God and wisdom.

The first few chapters of this section tell of the way in which God preserved Adam, judged Cain, destroyed the wicked with a flood, turned Lot's wife into a pillar of salt, and punished the unrighteous Canaanites. An example of this kind of writing comes from the story of Jacob.

> When a righteous man fled from his brother's wrath, she [wisdom] guided him on straight paths; she showed him the kingdom of God, and gave him knowledge of holy things; she prospered him in his labors, and increased the fruit of his toil. When his oppressors were covetous, she stood by him and made him rich. She protected him from his enemies, and kept him safe from those who lay in wait for him; in his arduous conflict she gave him the victory so that he might learn that godliness is more powerful than anything else. (10:10-12)

The later chapters consist of an extended prayer into which the author blended warnings against idolatry. It seems that one of his purposes was to address the Jews living in Egypt to warn them against the idolatrous ways of the Egyptians who, as he pointed out, were engaged in the absolute folly of worshiping stars, rivers, objects of gold or silver, or even departed loved ones as if they were gods who could help them.

> For the idea of making idols was the beginning of fornication, and the invention of them was the corruption of life, for they did not exist from the beginning, nor will they last forever. For through human vanity they entered the world, and therefore their speedy end has been planned. For a father, consumed with grief at an untimely bereavement, made an image of his child, who had been suddenly taken from him, he now honored as a god what was once a dead human being, and handed on to his dependents secret rites and initiations. (14:12-15)

Idolaters are people living in darkness. In contrast God's "holy ones" live with a "very great light." (18:1) As one of God's "holy ones" the apocryphal author prayed for those living in idolatry and he praised God for his great mercy.

> For all people who were ignorant of God were foolish by nature; and they were unable from the good things that are seen to know the one who exists, nor did they recognize the artisan while paying heed to the works; but they supposed that either fire or wind or swift air, or the circle of the stars, or turbulent water, or the luminaries of heaven are the gods that rule the world. If through delight in the beauty of these things people assumed them to be gods, let them know how much better than these is their Lord. (13:1-3)

> But you, our God, are kind and true, patient, and ruling all things in mercy. For even if we sin, we are yours, knowing your power; but we will not sin because we know that you acknowledge us as yours. For to know you is complete righteousness, and to know your power is the root of immortality. (15:1-3)

The Book concludes with a final word of gratitude to God.

> For in everything, O Lord, you have exalted and glorified your people, and have not neglected to help them at all times and in all places. (19:22)

Summary

Although neither author of the apocryphal books of wisdom knew Jesus, it is possible to read their books as Old Testament expressions of Jesus' summary of the Law of God in Matthew 22:37-40. Jesus said, "Love your neighbor as yourself." Those interpersonal relationships were the concern of Jesus Sirach. In summarizing the Law Jesus also said, "Love the Lord your God." In personifying wisdom and warning against idols the author of *Wisdom* had his mind on the God of Israel. "Neighbor" is the focus of The *Wisdom of Jesus Sirach*. God" is the focus of *The Book of Wisdom*.

Things to Think About

In what very specific ways can we "love God with our heart, our soul, our mind"? In what specific ways can we "love our neighbor"? In what specific ways can we love ourselves? Read I John 4:7-21. How is our love for God related to his love for us? How is our love for our neighbor related to our love for God?

Why did the Egyptians and the Canaanites think that they needed idols? Do you think that everybody needs some kind of god to worship, no matter how foolish it may seem to be? If so, why is that? What are contemporary idols that attract you? Why do you find them attractive?

Distinguish between knowledge and wisdom. How do we gain knowledge? How do we gain wisdom? Which is more difficult, and why?

The Apocryphal Legends, Part One

The apocryphal legends may be thought of as historical fiction. They are historical because they relate to people or events that are part of Israel's recorded history. Yet the stories are fictitious elaborations for which there is no biblical or extra-biblical support. The legends were written in the intertestamental period about events that the anonymous authors imagined had happened hundreds of years earlier.

The five legends tell stories about two events in Israel's history. The books of Tobit and Judith relate to the Assyrian captivity of Israel around 730 B.C. The remaining three books tell stories about Daniel and the Babylonian captivity around 580 B.C.

Tobit

Solomon was king over Israel around 950 B.C. When he died, the leadership of the kingdom went to his son Rehoboam. Under the strict measures of Rehoboam, the northern tribes of Israel rallied under Jeroboam and made him their king. Thus the twelve tribes of Israel were now divided with ten northern tribes as the Kingdom of Israel, and the remaining two tribes as the southern Kingdom of Judah. (I Kings 12)

Assyria was the major world power of the day. Around 750 B.C. it began a successful campaign against the northern Kingdom of Israel. By 732 B.C. Assyria was deporting Israeli captives to Assyria. Many of them settled in Assyria's capital city of Nineveh. Among them was Tobit from the tribe of Naphtali.

The tribe of Naphtali was known to be among the most idolatrous tribes of Israel. In spite of the wickedness of his neighbors, Tobit had remained true to the faith of his fathers. Before being taken into captivity he had regularly made the approximate 100 mile journey south to observe the Jewish festivals in Jerusalem. This was his testimony.

> I, Tobit, walked in the way of truth and righteousness all the days of my life. I performed many acts of charity for my kindred and my people who had gone with me in exile to Nineveh, in the land of the Assyrians. When I was in my own country, in the land of Israel, I was still a young man, the whole tribe of my ancestor Naphtali deserted the house of David and Jerusalem. This city had been chosen from among all the tribes of Israel, where all the tribes of Israel should offer sacrifice and where the temple, the dwelling of God, had been consecrated and established for all generations forever. All my kindred and our ancestral house of Naphtali sacrificed to the calf that King Jeroboam of Israel had erected in Dan and on all the mountains of Galilee. But I alone went often to Jerusalem for

the festivals, as it is prescribed for all Israel by an everlasting decree. (1:3-6a)

In his Assyrian captivity Tobit continued his faithfulness to the Lord and the Lord prospered him. He apparently became one of the trusted exiles in the service of the authorities. He gained considerable wealth and enjoyed freedom to travel. On one of his trips to Media (modern day northern Iran) he entrusted some of his wealth to a relative who lived there. Back in Nineveh Tobit married the pious Anna. They gave birth to a son and named him Tobias.

One day Tobit was sleeping in his garden when one of the sparrow droppings fell into his eyes and he became blind. He felt that his life was near its end. But before he died he decided that he must tell his son Tobias about the silver that was stored in Media. He asked Tobias to go to Media to retrieve the family wealth. Tobias agreed to go, but he had this problem.

> Then Tobias answered his father Tobi "I will do everything that you have commanded me, father, but how can I obtain the money from him [the family relative in Media], since he does not know me and I do not know him? Also, I do not know the roads to Media or how to get there." (5:1-2)

Enter Raphael, an angel who was disguised as a relative of the family. He said that he knew the relative and the way to Media. He offered to guide Tobias to Media. So Tobias and Raphael said goodbye to Tobit and Anna, and began the trek to Media. The first night out, they camped at the Tigris River.

> So they both [Tobias and Raphael] journeyed along and when the first night overtook them they camped by the Tigris river. Then the young man went down to wash his feet in the Tigris River. Suddenly a large fish leaped up from the water and tried to swallow the young man's foot, and he cried out. But the angel said to the young man, "Catch hold of the fish and hang on to it." So the young man grasped the fish and threw it up on the land. Then the angel said to him, "Cut open the fish and take out its gall, heart, and liver. Keep them all with you, but throw away the intestines. For the gall, heart, and liver are useful for medicine." So after cutting open the fish, the young man gathered together the gall, heart, and liver; then he roasted and ate some of the fish, and kept some to be salted. (6:2-6)

The next day they arrived at the home of a relative, not the one who had the money. This relative had a beautiful daughter named Sarah. She had been married seven times, and each time her husband died on the night of the wedding. As a result, Sarah became depressed. Tobias was the next relative in line so he had an obligation to marry Sarah according to the Law of Moses. Tobias was understandably apprehensive about marrying the beautiful, but apparently deadly Sarah. He did not want to be next victim.

Raphael told Tobias not to be afraid. The problem had been a demon in the marriage chamber on the night of the wedding. In order to get rid of the demon and cure Sarah of her depression this is what Raphael told Tobias to do.

> When you enter the bridal chamber, take some of the fish's liver and heart and put them on the embers of the incense. An odor will be given off; the demon will smell it and flee, and will never be seen near her any more. (6:17-18a)

And that is what happened. The terrible odor drove the demon away and cured Sarah's depression. The young couple enjoyed the first night of marriage. The wedding celebration lasted two weeks. During that time, Raphael went on to Media to recover the family's silver. By the time the wedding celebration ended, Raphael had returned from Media with the wealth and they were ready to return to Nineveh.

On the journey back, Raphael remembered that Tobit was blind and needed to be healed before he died. He said to Tobias:

> I know that his eyes will be opened. Smear the gall of the fish on his eyes, the medicine will make the white film shrink and peel from his eyes, and your father will regain his sight and will see the light. (11:7b-8)

And so the story ends. Raphael, Tobias and Sarah finally arrived in Nineveh where they were warmly welcomed by Anna. Tobias rubbed the fish's gall bladder into his father's eyes, and Tobit ass able to see. He embraced his son and praised God for healing. Raphael revealed that he was really an angel sent from God. Tobit told his son to take the wealth and leave Nineveh because God was going to destroy it. Tobit and Anna both died. Tobias buried them, and then headed back East with his father's money to live in comfort with the lovely Sarah.

Is there a meaning to the story? Several theories have been suggested. The name Raphael means "God heals." Could the name of the angel be the connection to the medicinal qualities of the decaying liver, heart, and gall bladder of the fish? Or is the message of the story that the God who created is the God who will provide. Or did the apocryphal author write this story to encourage the people of his day. When this book was written in the second century B.C. the faithful in Israel were dealing with the corrupting demands of Antiochus Epiphanes. The legend of Tobit might have been written to give Israel hope that the God who had delivered Israel from Assyria some 500 years earlier would deliver them from the Syrians now.

Whatever may have been the motive of the author the story is bathed in Jewish piety. Several prayers enrich the book, such as this prayer of Tobi.

> Then Tobit said, "Blessed be God who lives forever, because his kingdom lasts throughout all ages. For he afflicts, and he bestows mercy; he leads down to Hades in the lowest regions of the earth, and he brings up from the great abyss, and there is nothing that can escape his hand. (13:1-2)

> As for me, I exalt my God and my soul rejoices in the King of heaven. Let all people speak of his majesty, and acknowledge him in Jerusalem. O Jerusalem, the holy city, he afflicted you for the deeds of your hands, but will again have mercy on the children of the righteous." (13:7-9)

The piety that characterized Tobit surely rubbed off on his son Tobias. As beautiful as Sarah was, and as much as Tobias had confidence in Raphael's advice about the fish's heart and liver, Tobias refused to go to the marriage bed until he and Sarah stood and prayed together.

> When the parents had gone out and shut the door, Tobias got out of bed and said to Sarah, "Sister, get up, and let us pray and implore the Lord that he grant us mercy and safety." So she got up and they began to pray and implore that they might be kept safe. Tobias began by saying, "Blessed are you, O God of our ancestors, and blessed is your name in all generations forever. Let the heavens and the whole creation bless you forever. (8:4-5)
>
> I now am taking this kinswoman of mine, not because of lust, but with sincerity. Grant that she and I may find mercy and that we may grow old together." (8:7)

Judith

After Assyria had conquered the northern tribes of Israel it set its sights on the southern Kingdom of Judah and its capital city Jerusalem. The failed attempt to conquer Jerusalem is the setting for the book of Judith. It is possible that the apocryphal author took inspiration for his story from the centuries earlier account of Jael who drove a tent spike through the head of the Canaanite general Sisera, giving Israel the victory. (Judges 4:21)

The story moves slowly for the first few chapters. Nebuchadnezzar, who is named as the King of Assyria at that time, appointed General Holofernes to move West with the army from Nineveh towards the Mediterranean Sea to conquer all the land for Assyria. In particular, he was to make sure that the gods of these lands were destroyed.

> ... he had been commissioned to destroy the gods of the land, so that all nations should worship Nebucchadnezzar alone, and that all their dialects and tribes should call upon him as a god. (3:8b)

When they came to Palestine Holofernes heard that Judea and Jerusalem had set up effective defenses. He asked an informant to describe the people of Judea. The informant rehearsed the way in which Israel's God had delivered his people from Egypt and into the land of Canaan. He concluded by saying

> ... let my Lord [Holofernes] pass them by for their Lord and God will defend them, and we shall become the laughingstock of the whole world. (5:21)

The report did not please Holofernes,

> [You] tell us not to make war against the people of Israel because their God will defend them? What god is there except Nebuchadnezzar. He will send his forces and destroy them from the face of the earth. Their God will not save them. (6:2b)

So Holofernes led his troops South towards Jerusalem. They first had to conquer Bethulia, a town towards Jerusalem. Surrounding

Bethulia, they cut off the water supply and made it impossible for the residents to work their fields outside the town walls. The Israelites were terrified, and urged Uzzah, the city's mayor, to surrender to the Assyrians. He decided to wait five days, and if the Lord did not deliver them within those days, he would surrender to the Assyrians. (7:30)

At that point, Judith entered the story. She is described as a beautiful and fearless widow. She was very upset with Mayor Uzzah and the town elders because they had set a condition on God. If God failed to live up to their time table of five days, then they would surrender. So she called for a special meeting of the elders, and this is what she said:

> Listen to me, rulers of the people of Bethulia! What you have said to the people today is not right; you have even sworn and pronounced this oath between God and you, promising to surrender the town to our enemies unless the Lord turns and helps us within so many days. Who are you to put God to the test today, and to set ourselves up in the place of God in human affairs? You are putting the Lord Almighty to the test, but you will never learn anything! You cannot plumb the depths of the human heart or understand the workings of the human mind,; how do you expect to search out God who made all these things, and find out his mind or comprehend his thought? (8:11-14)

She requested and received permission to leave the city and appeal to the Assyrians. She prayed for divine wisdom and courage, and went down to the headquarters of the Assyrian army and asked to see General Holofernes. She flirted with him, got him drunk in his tent, and this is what happened then.

> [The guards all left.] but Judith was left alone in the tent, with Holofernes stretched out on his bed, for he was dead drunk. Now Judith had told her maid to stand outside the bedchamber and wait for her to come out, as she did on the other days; for she said she wanted to be going out for her prayers. She had said the same thing to Bagoas. So everyone went out, and no one, either small or great was left in the bedchamber. Then Judith, standing beside his bed, said in her heart, "O God of all might, look in this hour on the work of my hands for the exaltation of Jerusalem. Now indeed is the time to help your heritage and carry out my design to destroy the enemies who have risen up against us." She went up to the bedpost near Holofernes' head, and took down his sword that hung there. She came close to the bed, and took hold of the hair of his head, and said, "Give me strength today, O God of Israel!" Then she struck his neck twice with all her might, and cut off his head. Next she rolled his body on the bed and pulled down the canopy from the posts. Soon afterward she went out and gave Holofernes' head to her maid, who placed in in her food bag. (13:2-10)

With the death of the great General Holofernes, the Assyrian army was demoralized. They all fled, Israel rejoiced, and Judith composed a Psalm of praise.

I will sing to my God a new song: O Lord, you are great and glorious, wonderful in strength, invincible. Let all your creatures serve you, for you spoke, and they were made. You sent forth your spirit, and it formed them; there is none that can resist your voice. For the mountains shall be shaken to their foundations with the waters; before your glance the rocks shall melt like wax. But to those who fear you, you show mercy. (16:13-15)

Things to Think About

The Assyrian captivity obviously lived long in the memory of Israel. Are there any "memories that live long" as you think of your nation's history? The history of the church? Your own family or personal history?

Read Psalm 77:1-11. The Psalmist remembered significant events in the life of his people. So did the anonymous authors of Tobit and Judith. Do you sense any difference in the way in which David remembered, and the way in which Tobi and Judith remembered Israel's Assyrian captivity?

When Jael drove a tent spike through Sisera's head (Judges 4:21) Deborah sang a song of praise to God. (Judges 5:24-30) When Judith cut off the head of Holofernes she composed a Psalm of praise. What should be the Christian's response when a nation defeats an enemy?

THE APOCRYPHAL LEGENDS, PART TWO

The three remaining apocryphal legends all relate to the story of Daniel at the time of Israel's Babylonian captivity. The *Belgic Confession* names these as three separate books. As the listing of the apocryphal books on pages xiii and xiv shows, the Roman Catholic Douay version of Scripture, among others, incorporates these legends directly into the canonical book of Daniel. All three legends were written early in the Maccabean period between 200 and 150 B.C. when Israel treasured stories of its heroes from the past.

The Song of the Three Children

The Song of the Three Children is also known as The Song of the Three Jews. It has also been called the Prayer of Azariah. In some collections Azariah's prayer is separated from the Song so that the one book becomes two. The legend is about Daniel's three friends, Shadrach, Meshach, and Abednego. Abednego's Hebrew name was Azariah.

Canonical Daniel 3:23 reads, "The soldiers took Shadrach, Meshach, and Abednego, and these three men, firmly tied, fell into the blazing furnace." (NIV) At that point in the Roman Catholic Douay version's Song of the Three Children becomes an insertion of seventy verses. At the end of the insertion the story continues as it does in canonical Daniel at chapter 3:24 where it was reported to Nebuchadnezzar that not three, but four men were walking around in the furnace, apparently unscathed.

The first part of the book is the prayer of Azariah, or Abednego, who confessed Israel's sins that brought them into captivity. He pleaded for God's mercy. What follows is a sampling of his prayer.

> Blessed are you, O Lord, God of our ancestors, and worthy of praise; and glorious is your name forever! For you are just in all that you have done; all your works are true and your ways are just, and all your judgments are true. You have executed true judgments in all that you have brought upon us and upon Jerusalem, the holy city of our ancestors; by a true judgment you have brought all this upon us because of our sins. For we have sinned and broken your law in turning away from you; in all matters we have sinned grievously. (:3-6)

> Do not withdraw your mercy from us, for the sake of Abraham your beloved and for the sake of your servants Isaac and Israel. (:12)

The second and longest part of this book presumably occurred when the angel came to protect them from the flames. The song is really a psalm, structured in the pattern of Psalm 136 where we find the repeated refrain – "His love endures forever." In The Song of the

Three Children, we find a similar repetition of the phrases "Bless the Lord" and "Sing praise."

> Bless the Lord, all people on earth, sing praise to him and highly exalt him forever. Bless the Lord, O Israel, sing praise to him and highly exalt him forever. Bless the Lord, you priests of the Lord, sing praise to him and highly exalt him forever. Bless the Lord, you servants of the Lord, sing praise to him and highly exalt him forever. Bless the Lord, spirits and souls of the righteous, sing praise to him and highly exalt him forever. Bless the Lord, you who are holy and humble in heart, sing praise to him and highly exalt him forever. (:60-65)

<u>Susanna</u>

The apocryphal story of Susanna is sometimes placed as a second insertion into the book of Daniel. Canonical Daniel consists of twelve chapters. When the legend of Susanna is added it becomes chapter thirteen. Although the story is about Susanna, Daniel emerges as the hero. The opening verses introduce us to Susanna.

> There was a man living in Babylon whose name was Joakim. He married the daughter of Hilkiah, named Susanna, a very beautiful woman and one who feared the Lord. Her parents were righteous and had trained their daughter according to the law of Moses. Joakim was very rich and had a fine garden adjoining his house; the Jews used to come

to him because he was the most honored of them all. (:1-4)

The elders in the town, who were the judges, regularly met in Joakim's home to administer justice. Two of those elders began to lust after the beautiful Susanna and they schemed how they could seduce her.

> Once, while they were watching for an opportune day, she went in as before with only two maids, and wished to bathe in the garden, for it was a hot day. No one was there except the two elders, who had hidden themselves and were watching her. (:15-16)

> When the maids had gone out. the two elders got up and ran to her. They said, "Look, the garden doors are shut, and no one can see us. We are burning with desire for you, so give your consent, and lie with us. If you refuse, we will testify against you that a young man was with you, and this was why you sent your maids away." (:19-21)

The godly Susanna refused the sexual advances of these elders, and they fulfilled their threat. They held court, and accused her in front of the rest of the elders for having consensual sex under the trees in the garden. She was found guilty, and according to the Law of Moses she was sentenced to death. But this is what happened next.

> Then the Lord heard her cry. Just as she was being led off to execution, God stirred up the holy spirit of a young lad named Daniel, and he shouted with

a loud voice, "I want no part in the shedding of this woman's blood." (:44-46)

Back in court, Daniel separated the two elders and examined them one at a time. He asked the first elder: "Under what tree did they have sex?" The elder answered, "It was a mastic tree." After this brief testimony he was excused. Then the other elder came in. Daniel asked him the same question: "Under what tree did you see them having sex?" This elder answered, "It was an evergreen oak." (:54-58) The proof was there. The elders had born false witness against Susanna. This is how it ended.

> Then the whole assembly raised a great shout and blessed God, who saves those who hope in him. And they took action against the two elders, because out of their own mouths Daniel had convicted them of bearing false witness. They did to them as they had wickedly planned to do to their neighbor. Acting in accordance with the law of Moses, they put them to death. Thus innocent blood was spared that day. (:60-62)

The story concludes with the report that "from that day onward Daniel had a great reputation among the people." (:64)

Bell and the Dragon

This is the third apocryphal legend that relates to the story of Daniel. In the Douay version of Scripture the story of Bel and the

Dragon is added as chapter 14 to canonical Daniel. By this time in Israel's history Persia had defeated Babylon, and Cyrus, the Persian, was King. As is true in the biblical story, Cyrus thought highly of Daniel.

> Daniel was companion of the king, and was the most honored of all his Friends. (:2)

The biblical story of Daniel shows him to be fiercely loyal to Israel's God. In the imagination of the apocryphal author this loyalty stimulated debates with King Cyrus over whose god was greater: the god of the Persians or the living God of heaven and earth. The legend consists of three episodes that honor Daniel as the defender of the honor of Israel's God.

Episode one: Bel

In those days the god of Persia was a statue named Bel who lived in in its own temple and was served by seventy priests and their families. Every day a quantity of food was placed as an offering to Bel. Each morning of the next day the food was gone. This convinced Cyrus that Bel was such a great god that it needed its daily provisions of twelve bushels of fine flour, forty sheep, and six measures of wine. (:3)

Daniel laughed at this, so the king proposed a test. In the temple of Bel, the statue's daily rations would be laid out as usual. The door would be locked and sealed with the king's signet. If in the morning, the food was gone that would be proof that Bel had eaten it and Daniel would be killed for blaspheming Bel. If the food was still there proving that Bel had not eaten it, the priests of Bel would be killed. Daniel said to the king, "Let it be done as you have said." (:8-9)

The priests of Bel were not concerned about the contest because they had created a secret door into the temple where they regularly entered at night to steal the food that had been offered to Bel. They were confident that the food would be gone the next morning, their lives would be spared, and Daniel would be killed. But Daniel had a different idea.

> The king set out the food for Bel. Then Daniel ordered his servants to bring ashes, and they scattered them throughout the temple in the presence of the king alone. Then they went out, shut the door and sealed it with the king's signet, and departed. (:14)

That night, all unaware of the ashes on the floor, the priests, their wives, and children entered as usual and stole the food for themselves.

> Early in the morning the king rose and came, and Daniel with him. The king said, "Are the seals unbroken, Daniel?" He answered, "They are unbroken, O king." As soon as the doors were opened, the king looked at the table, and shouted with a loud voice, "You are great, O Bel, and in you there is no deceit at all." (:16)

Before the king could enter the temple, Daniel pointed to the floor. It was covered with footprints of men, women, and children who had come in through their secret door to steal the food.

> Then the king was enraged, and he arrested the priests and their wives and children. They showed him the secret door through which they used to enter to consume what was on the table. Therefore the king put them to death, and gave Bel over to Daniel, who destroyed it and its temple. (:21-22)

Episode two: the dragon

But now the Persians needed a new god. Daniel had boasted that his God was "the living God." So Cyrus decided that the Persians next god should be a living god. They found their new god in a great and fierce dragon.

> Now in that place there was a great dragon, which the Babylonians revered. The king said to Daniel, "You cannot deny that this is a living god, so worship him." Daniel said, "I worship the Lord my God, for he is the living God. But give me permission, O king, and I will kill the dragon without a sword or club." The king said, "I give you permission." (:23-26)

Daniel boiled pitch, fat, and hair. (:27) The strange mixture was designed to expand dramatically in the stomach resulting in an internal explosion. He made little cakes, and fed them to the dragon.

> The dragon ate them and burst open. Then Daniel said, "See what you have been worshiping!" (:27)

By now the Persians were very upset. Daniel, this exile from Israel, had destroyed two of their gods. So the people of Babylon conspired against the king, saying,

> The king has become a Jew; he has destroyed Bel and killed the dragon, and slaughtered the priests." Going to the king they said, "Hand Daniel over to us, or else we will kill you and your household." (:28-29)

The king relented and handed Daniel over to those who wanted to destroy him.

> They threw Daniel into the lion's den, and he was there for six days. There were seven lions in the den, and every day they had been given two human bodies and two sheep; but now they were given nothing, so that they would devour Daniel. (:31-32)

Episode three: the lion's den

The third episode in this legend is the apocryphal author's imagination of the way in which God took care of Daniel in the lion's den. For six days the unfed, hungry lions did not touch Daniel. They were hungry, but so was Daniel.

In those days the prophet Habakkuk was living in Jerusalem. One evening he was preparing a stew that he would take to the reapers who were working in his fields when he had this remarkable experience.

> But the angel of the Lord said to Habakkuk, "Take the food that you have to Babylon, to Daniel, in the lions' den. Habakkuk said, "Sir, I have never seen Babylon, and I know nothing about the den." Then the angel of the Lord took him by the crown of his head and carried him by his hair; with the speed of the wind he set him down in Babylon, right over the den. Then Habakkuk said, "Daniel, Daniel! Take the food that God has sent you." Daniel said, "You have remembered me, O God, and have not forgotten those who love you." So Daniel got up and ate. And the angel of God immediately returned Habakkuk to his own place. (:34-39)

The apocryphal legend ends as does in the canonical story. The king praised Daniel's God, and had the enemies thrown into the lion's den where they were devoured.

Things to Think About

Reflect on the fourteen books of The Apocrypha. Are there any that you wish would have been included in the canon of the Old Testament? Any that you are glad were not?

In general these books were written between the end of the Old Testament and the beginning of the New. What have you learned about the people of Israel during those years that are sometimes called "the silent years."?

Has the study of the books of The Apocrypha enriched your faith? Challenged it? Disturbed it? Explain.

We might think of John Bunyan's *Pilgrim's Progress*, and C. S. Lewis's *Screwtape Letters* as legends that are related to biblical material. They are not offered as part of the canon of Scripture, but are there any similarities between them and the Old Testament Apocrypha?

CPSIA information can be obtained at www.ICGtesting.com
Printed in the USA
BVOW09s0617041214

377644BV00001B/2/P